Renouncing Violence

Mary Margaret Funk, OSB

D1496207

LITURGICAL PRESS

Collegeville, Minnesota

www.litpress.org

1   2   3   4   5   6   7   8   9

Library of Congress Cataloging-in-Publication Data

Names: Funk, Mary Margaret, author.
Title: Renouncing violence / Mary Margaret Funk, OSB.
Description: Collegeville, Minnesota : Liturgical Press, 2018. |
    Includes bibliographical references.
Identifiers: LCCN 2018004772 (print) | LCCN 2018032107 (ebook) |
    ISBN 9780814684849 (ebook) | ISBN 9780814684597
Subjects: LCSH: Violence—Religious aspects—Christianity. |
    Nonviolence—Religious aspects—Christianity.
Classification: LCC BT736.15 (ebook) | LCC BT736.15 .F86 2018
    (print) | DDC 241/.697—dc23
LC record available at https://lccn.loc.gov/2018004772.

To those who fetch, bless, and are blessed by Holy Water

Contents

Acknowledgments

My thanks to my superior, Sister Jennifer Mechtild Horner, OSB, and my community, especially Sister Harriet Woehler, OSB, Sister Mary Sue Freiberger, OSB, Sister Mary Kay Greenawalt, OSB, and Sister Ann Patrice Papesh, OSB.

Special gratitude goes to Colleen Mathews, a generous collaborator. Other contributors include Mary Collins, OSB, Bob Eisenhut, Leo Lefebure, Kathleen Cahalan, Mary Margaret Heintzkill, Loraine Brown, William Skudlarek, OSB, Dan Ward, OSB, Elias Deitz, OCSO, Lawrence Morey, OCSO, Sara Wuthnow, Joyce Weller, DC, Bridget Funk, Dr. Catherine Hindle, Dick Funk, Dr. Tom Funk, OD, Mark Nowak, Theresa and Hal Schoen, Judith Valente, Patrick Cooney, OSB, Judith Cebula, Laura Klauberg, Carolyn Benner, Marina C. Funk, Mairin Ni Fhlaithearta, Jim Farrell, Dr. Gale Rutan, Dr. Joseph Francis, Gregory Escardo, OCSO, and Patrick Hart, OCSO.

Hans Christoffersen, publisher at Liturgical Press, made this book happen. Beyond dialogue, he brought writing toward literature.

Preface

"Violence" needs no introduction. *Renouncing* violence needs a whole book. The intent of this book is to gentle down. Calmness prevents and scatters violence. When violence is tamed, we find peace of heart. A working definition of violence is "form or forces that cause harm." We can do something about violence. I've known that there's no wrath in God, no anger in Jesus, and that we have the Holy Spirit to help us. So why, then, is facing violence and refraining from contributing to the cycle of violence so hard? We can ever so confidently take the opportunity to pause and properly respond rather than react. This book can help us proceed with confidence. Through renunciation, both individually and together, we can reduce, redirect, refrain, and reprogram our instinctual propensities toward retaliation, recompense, and rage.

How I Came to Write This Book

The *first phase* was listening and hearing that something new was happening these recent years. Too many people, too often, were reporting their bouts of fear and doubt. The new normal was anxiety from within and fear from without. Oppositional soundbites prevail. Gaps of silence shout at the dinner table. Numbness has fogged over conversations.

The *second phase* was pausing myself and listening to my own disquietude. During the summer of 2016 I watched the PBS evening news summary of both the Republican and Democratic conventions. By election day in November I realized that I was saturated with the affliction of anger. I got permission to make a retreat with Sister Catherine Griffiths, SNDdeN. In February 2017, I flew to Boston, made my way to Ipswich, and stayed with Sister Catherine for a week at the provincial house of the Sisters of Notre Dame de Namur. This eighty-three-year-old nun prayed out my anger. I realize most souls don't have a Sister Catherine. I also realize that I was not cleansed for my lifetime. I needed to guard my heart lest anger return, bringing seven more demons stronger than the first.

The *third phase* was waiting on the Spirit to direct me to something I should do about this new normal. We are in a global bad mood. What in our tradition would be helpful for us in these times? I realized that my own anger paralyzed me from taking discerned action. I've had an ongoing practice of *lectio divina*. I gradually encountered[1] my received tradition. I found compelling evidence that Jesus reversed violence through his death and resurrection, that there is no anger in Jesus, only love. He came to complete creation. I also found solid evidence that there is no wrath in God and that the church was commissioned to extend the reign of peace and well-being in this life and the next. This message is a stunning, solid foundation that helps me to be firmly confident in my faith, both as a way into the action of believing and a way to know the substance or content of my faith claims. This sound Christian tradition that I discovered through *lectio divina* eclipsed some earlier formation that presented me with content to the contrary.

These three phases converged with significant conversations, especially with Hans Christoffersen, publisher at Liturgical Press, that prompted me to write a proposal for this book, *Renouncing Violence*.

The sweep of the book came easily. Some chapters needed several drafts, but the content was never stuck or without compelling sources, which I share in footnotes. I've attached a rather hefty bibliography for readers who want to do their own homework on this earlier monastic tradition. It's only recently that these classic sources have become so widely available in English and in reader-friendly translations.

Structure of This Book

Chapter 1: About Renunciation

First, I look at the why of renunciation. To get out of the cycle of violence we employ a countermotion that checks aggression and replaces unconscious reaction with discerned response. Between the impulse and the response are poise and endless possibilities. Renouncing is the opportunity to change and lift up toward God for the common good. We respond with a root action deeply benefitting our domain of the humble human. How we know what to renounce is to find our vocation, our way of life. Then we renounce what is not a good fit for our designated calling for this lifetime. I share a method of renunciation that I know through the monastic tradition. When our way of life is renunciation, then it's natural to renounce violence. Renouncing is a poised but active way of living. We pause and then lean in to the right and good rather than react from our default defenses.

Chapter 2: About Jesus

Jesus initiates us into the reign of God. We imitate Jesus by healing harm today like he did in his historical times. This chapter has three parts that examine closely the historical life of Jesus. We encounter how the early church and those who knew him as Jesus of Nazareth told the story of Jesus.

Part 1 lists twenty-two pericopes (distinct passages) of healing. Jesus is the revelation of a new time when all will be well. Jesus is our way out of violence and into the reign of God that begins now and goes on for all eternity.

Part 2 considers the often-asked question, "Was Jesus angry?" through an exegesis of the four gospel passages that report Jesus' cleansing of the temple. Through careful study we see that, in Jesus, there is no wrath. This incident is often used to justify angry reactions that harm others. Jesus did no harm; he only healed. The four reports in the four gospels give four versions of Jesus doing symbolic action on behalf of the new reign of God. Jesus is the new temple dwelling among us (John 2:19).

Part 3 lingers with the passion narrative. So many details of that profound event report that Jesus could have reacted with destructive emotions and what is called "righteous" justified anger. Yet, in every account, he was measured and used the tragedy to extend compassion.

Jesus overwhelmingly healed and endured suffering for our sakes. He loves us very much, especially the most vulnerable ones among us. We conclude that there is no anger in Jesus. There is no evidence that he rains down the wrath of God, but there are numerous stories about his healing ministry. This teaching is important because if we see Jesus as a wrathful human it justifies anger and retaliation in our personal and social disputes.

Chapter 3: About How God Has No Wrath

Although the biblical literature uses anthropomorphic images, there is no wrath in God. God created us out of love, sustains us, and continues creation in us. This chapter gave me an opportunity to manifest my own creedal statement of death and what happens after. What do I believe? For some years I used Julian of Norwich as my revelatory text for sustained *lectio*. Her teachings are a transmission for me. I found that her voice was my own deepest self. This *lectio* is how this book became a teaching on renouncing violence. It makes sense to align our beliefs about God, our deepest sensitivities in our hearts, and do the humble work of inner reconciliation. The progression continues: if there is no anger in Jesus and no wrath in God, then what? I have every reason to be confident in this God who holds me in the grasp of love, not only because this is my own near-death experience,[2] but also because this too is the experience of others. The moment of death especially reveals God's love.

Chapter 4: About How God So Loves the World

Jesus breathed on his disciples the Holy Spirit to give us a profound peace. I examine John 20:17, on forgiveness. The cause of Jesus' in-breaking into our world was to continue the creation that is the fulfillment of Love. In John's account, we do not find the themes that postulate Jesus' incarnation, death, and resurrection as atonement, expiation, reparation, justice, or sacrificial offering. Jesus came and dwelt among us. This is God loving the world so much that the Son was sent from all eternity. This good news is critical for us today. We have the revelation to move from violence to peace. Renouncing violence attends to this Easter experience in the Gospel of John. This Fourth Gospel confirms that is there is no wrath in God and no anger in Jesus. The Great Commission is to extend this reign of God (Matt 29:19). Even now this has already begun.

Chapter 5: About Discernment

Through the action of the Holy Spirit we know when, how, where, and with whom to respond in the face of violence. The way forward is to renounce violence. Then, through discernment, we find the skillful means of sorting out right action so that there is the surge of God's presence that replaces harm with healing and replenishes nature with peace. We not only do the right action but also act out of a right intention and motivation so that we continue the ministry of Christ in our times like he did two thousand years ago.

How does that practice of discernment work? I share one example of discerning what is the question and the appropriate response. I use the story of writing this book. I'm demonstrating how the process of discernment works.

Chapter 6: About Anger

We encounter obstacles to hearing the still, small voice of the Holy Spirit. For me, my dominant obstacle is anger. In this chapter, I tell the story of my own anger regarding a dispute with a chaplain. He was my foe, but, by the grace of God, he became my friend. Other people have other afflictions, like greed or depression, but for me it is anger. The story gives witness that through prayer we can get on the other side of anger, root it out. Then it is imperative to be vigilant.

Chapter 7: About Practice

Renouncing violence is training the mind to move like a muscle, not acquiring more content for the thinking mind. This is a learned skill that requires the kind of practice one does when learning Zen, yoga, music, or a new language. There's direct encoding and patterning of brain pathways. There are also ways into the heart through training the mind. We can change both as individuals and as distinct communities. This chapter brings forward the desert tradition of contemplative living.

Chapter 8: About Holy Water

This chapter is simply an invitation to use holy water. The observance of holy water creates zones of peace through the sign and gesture of the cross. We say this prayer: "In the name of the Father, the Son, and the Holy Spirit." The sacramental usage of holy water is a received tradition. We can be confident that through faith this holy water blesses, purifies, and preserves this ongoing conversion into the reign of God where harms are healed and evil is prevented. We notice the prescribed prayers used to bless ordinary water, then we join our faith with the ancient blessings of the devout. We appropriate the use of holy water ourselves in our own gestures of blessings. This revelation gives us confidence that holy water is a way forward to replace harm with healing, doubt with confidence, and fear with peace.

This book intends to show how the Holy Spirit directs us. We renounce our ways of living that cause harm. We, ever so gently, by the Holy Spirit, respond with deliberately chosen actions. What comes with discernment is also the actual grace to renounce violence. The gesture of using holy water embodies our prayer that Father, Son, and Holy Spirit purify, bless, and sanctify, thereby reversing violence and revealing love.

This book includes a holy water prayer that is easy to memorize:[3]

Father, Son, and Spirit
Through these sacred waters,
calm, heal, hold,
Now and Forever. Amen.

Chapter One

About Renunciation

Renunciation is the essential, elemental, and simple expression of one's vocation, one's calling. For me, it was to be a nun. And then the graces of that calling were provided. So, it was not the strenuous, sacrificial, blood-wrenching, searing, hemorrhaging of just grasping for my own desires. There is something very natural and noble about finding a fit and stepping up to its requirements. I've seen it in marriages and in people who have dedicated themselves to a single life. I've also seen it in people who have various sequential stages of a vocation because of circumstances. I have witnessed inner strength and resilience to step into one's vocation to shoulder the consequent responsibilities.

My vocation to be a nun required renouncing other options that would have been another way of life. Being a nun is a specific way of life, not just a lifestyle that has phases that are sporadic and casual. Being a nun is the whole of my life, *all* of my life.

In the early 1970s, church law gave Benedictine sisters the option to make the solemn vow of total renunciation. The intent behind this particular legal expression of the vow of poverty was a stricter interpretation regarding one's opportunity to acquire property. This rigorous vow governs all things that the individual nun may have brought with her from her former way of life, that might come her way at the death of her parents, or that she acquires through some other income stream. All income would automatically become property of the monastery. The individual sister would have no executive power to receive, use, or redistribute things.

How this works practically is that all goods are held in common. Through permissions of the superior, each sister is given the things that are necessary for her well-being and work. A system of accountability, permissions, and blessings of obedience replaces the economics of owning, possessing, and distributing things. It is a total renunciation not to have exclusive personal power over things. In fact, it's to not *have* things but to *use* things with the blessing of obedience.

While this may sound strict, it was a grace-filled moment when I signed my papers. I remember talking with the lawyer who drew up these agreements and got us aligned with both civil and canon law. He sat back in his chair and said, "Well, this is nothing different than the way my wife and I hold things together for the sake of the family."

Renunciation is a way of good order to direct one's individual preferences, and desires, and ways of holding things in common for the sake of the common good, that is, the family or the community. Renunciation is a way for the individual to have good order. Renunciation is also a way to focus one's energies. It is fitting to have one's deepest desires met. Renunciation is also an opportunity to go beyond oneself for the sake of others. It is sweet to take on responsibilities that ensure other people's desires are fulfilled, maybe even at some sacrifice. There's a sweet spot when vocation is at work and at the same time making a difference for others.

Renunciation, in and of itself, will seem to have a missing piece if, indeed, there isn't an overarching and underpinning belief. The why of renunciation is the result of having a calling, a vocation from God. We discover our calling and then follow our heart's desire. At some point, we decide and reside in that "good fit." This place where I live in my own skin feels solid and right. Vocation is like a good pair of walking shoes. It fits so well you walk without being aware of your feet. Sometimes it's not the shoes (my vocation) that has been tough, but the terrain. I've had some years where the trail was obscure, the passages narrow and steep. The monastic way of life could give Tibetan Sherpas pause. Monastic life tends toward high-minded striving that can be extremely risky. Even in recent years I've suffered from delusional aspirations of my own making. Humility takes my hubris seriously. I smile more at this "work in progress."

After we accept and know our vocation, we renounce all manner of our former ways of life. This is different for each person. What is God for someone else? God's will for them? God's way for them? God's way is what we call "vocation." The *before* that existed before realizing my vocation is no longer my heart's desire, my way toward God. I am called to renounce all that is not God even if it might be a good for someone else. I renounce anything that is not God for me.

Renunciation, whether or not it is a vow, as in the monastic life or marriage, has accompanying benefits. First, it relaxes me into being who I am. I have a radar that knows when I am off-center, off-message. A second benefit of renunciation is that I feel confident that, through my way of life, I support other people's way of life, both by example and by using only the resources I need so that there are resources for others. I renounce grasping. I don't need anything more. A third benefit of renunciation is that there is a sweetness about having only what I need, living the life of the early church in the Acts of the Apostles where each one is given what they need, and following the Rule of Benedict, which says, "and be not grieved if someone needs more."[1]

An Opportunity to Practice Renunciation

Some thirty years ago in our monastery we were permitted to have a little television in our rooms. It was understood that nuns would watch wholesome programs. This practice of a personal television would not even have been considered before Vatican II, but with the softer interpretation of rules, televisions infiltrated the monastery. We're talking about little, tiny TVs. Nuns would watch sports or news or some cozy programs. I had a little Panasonic television that I had brought home from Catholic University when I was living in a dormitory as a graduate student.

One time, I fell asleep with it on and woke up with the volume too loud for the hall. I also looked at it and said, "This is nothing I would watch." And it was very easy and very natural, I remember, to unplug my television and take it down to the infirmary where sisters would welcome a device to use when sick. I never looked back; I never had a television in my room after that. I realized that the TV was part of my former way of life as a student.

When I let it go, I realized how much more peace I had in my space. I could recover the idea and the meaning of a cell, which is not for entertainment: it's for prayer, it's for good order, and it's for silence. And more than that, I realized that indiscriminate watching of television was harmful to my calm mind, especially commercials. It's not that I watched bad programs, but it was too loud, too much, too exciting, and away from a calm, listening presence in my cell. Sometimes I accompanied somebody else and watched a program or I targeted something specific to watch, but as such, I renounced television. And the other side of not having that noise is that there are no triggers to return to my former way of life. Renouncing television calmed my mind.

This detachment gave me more agency that I can do this or that or not. I could look at a program or not look at a program to be free from any addictions of "Oh, that's my night for this program." When that lifted, when I had no programs that I needed to watch or see, it was like sitting on a porch swing in a very gentle breeze. So, renunciation is a sweet opportunity to reclaim one's vocation of a well-ordered and happily directed consciousness. Renunciation is the opportunity for well-ordered time, place, space, things, and relationships: energies in readiness.

When I was privileged to be part of a delegation from the Monastic Dialogue Board, we met with the Dalai Lama in Dharamsala, India. Some years ago, he said that the Tibetan word for monk was "to be content." Another word for a monastic is a "renunciate." This is obviously a fine description for those of us in the monastic way of life. Yet, it seems to me that it is also fine for my three brothers and two sisters. All of them—whether married with family, single with children, or gay—have made choices that focus their vocation.

A New Practice within "The Practice"

A singular grace came my way at the inception of writing this book. I accepted an invitation that seemed to come from a very deep place in my heart: "Write the book using the practice of renouncing violence." Immediately I took up what seemed to be a new practice for me, that is, to do this project accompanied as much as possible with a distinct practice: I'd stop when eyes signaled fatigue; I went for a walk sooner rather than later in the afternoon to give comfort to tense muscles; I yielded to getting a cup of decaf coffee or herbal tea no matter what time of day or night. When I noticed entanglements, as in fussing with the content, I'd shut the book or ask the callers on the other end of my phone if I could call them back later. In short, the process was to renounce anxiety, confusion, intensity and replace those moments with calm attention, quiet prayer, relaxed body and mind. The practice was to be calm, gently attentive with a steady writing pace punctuated by poise, pausing often for peace. This practice was not limited to my mind but also to the way I touched my computer, paged books, searched in the library or referenced the Scriptures for that perfect quote and accurate citation. Renouncing violence was a personal invitation and I was surprised how easily the opportunities invited me to shift from aggression to collaboration with time, things, and even conceptual abstractions. The book was long gone to the publisher, but this practice was stated specifically on my *Bona Opera* (resolutions for Lent based on good works, prayer, and fasting), submitted on Ash Wednesday for a Lenten resolution, blessed by my superior. So, renouncing violence came to be a way of life, not just another book!

Renunciation is a skillful way of living, but how does it address the forms and forces that cause harm? Is there a way out of the cycle of violence? The next chapter is about Jesus. We can entrust ourselves to live into the revelation that Jesus reverses harm and that healing happens.

Chapter Two

About Jesus, the Way out of Violence

Violence reigns when the middle way is no longer holding the center. Renunciation as a way of life allows us to stay on message and live toward God. This is our vocation, a calling. We each have a vocation, but sometimes it's hidden. My vocation as a nun is explicitly visible, but I can't do it by myself. Our vocation, whatever our calling, is not a cold, sterile combat with guts and grit. We have a personal and felt experience of being on the journey with someone. This someone is Jesus. Violence undermines our steady journey toward God. Jesus is the way out of the cycle of violence.

Jesus was an actual historical person living on our planet. He was born during the reign of King Herod. He lived in an actual place, Nazareth in the region of Galilee, with family and friends. He was a respected Jewish teacher. In this chapter we will see how the biblical narrative reveals Jesus as the Suffering Servant whose love in action heals rather than harms. We will see Jesus standing in the long line of prophets whose prophetic action shows his mission to restore all people to God through relationship with him. In this chapter we will see Jesus clearly rejects violence as he concludes his earthly mission, even as he yields to the violence enacted on him in his passion and death.

Jesus as Healer

There are more than twenty stories of Jesus healing people in the gospels. He heals men and women, sons and daughters, Jews and Gentiles. His healings are at once physical and spiritual. The blind gain more than their sight; they see Jesus as their Lord and Savior. The deaf regain more than their hearing; they hear the voice of Jesus and follow him in faith. Let's look now at each of the healing stories in the gospels.[1]

In the eighth chapter of Matthew's gospel, after Jesus gives the Sermon on the Mount, there is a series of healings. A large crowd follows Jesus, and he attracts those in need of healing, those who see him as the source of life and wholeness. Jesus reaches out to a leper and proclaims his desire to heal this man living in the margins of human society (Matt 8:1-4). Astonished at the centurion's faith in his ability to heal, Jesus cures the centurion's paralyzed servant from a distance (Matt 8:5-13). Jesus restores Peter's mother-in-law who is ill with a fever (Matt 8:14-15) and then heals many others who are possessed by demons or other maladies (Matt 8:16-17).

Matthew's gospel in particular links Jesus' healing ministry with his passion and death. His healings fulfill Isaiah's Suffering Servant prophecy and show his deep experience of human infirmity and disease (Matt 8:1-17 and Isa 53:4). When Jesus heals the man with the withered hand on the Sabbath, the Pharisees take offense at the healing and begin to plot to destroy him (Matt 12:9-14). In contrast to the violence in the hearts of the Pharisees, Jesus is the Suffering Servant, the one who doesn't harm, breaking neither a bruised reed nor a smoldering wick. Yet he brings justice and healing, even to those outside of Israel (Matt 12:12-21). Jesus himself uses the language of the passion and suffering to describe his ministry, saying he came not to be served but to serve and to give up his life for others (Matt 20:28).

Jesus raises the dead three times. First, Jesus meets a funeral procession in the city of Nain (Luke 7:11-17). A young man has died, leaving his widowed mother alone. She is weeping over the loss of her son, her sorrow made worse by the destitution she now faces. Jesus, deeply moved by her misery, tells the widow not to weep. He touches the coffin, halts the procession, and speaks to the young man, telling him to rise. The young man rises, and Jesus restores this beloved son to his mother. The crowd watches and erupts in praises to God.

Jesus raises Jairus's daughter from the dead after Jairus comes to him to beg for help for his dying daughter (Mark 5:22-24, 34-43). Jairus is with Jesus when he gets word that his daughter has died. Jesus goes to the dead girl, assuring Jairus and telling him not to fear but to believe. Skeptical mourners laugh at Jesus when he tells them that the child is not dead but sleeping. Jesus, however, takes the girl by the hand and tells her to rise and, again, all who see the healing are amazed.

The story of Lazarus is the third story where Jesus raises someone from the dead (John 11:1-41). This account works on two levels. One level is the physical death and restoration of Lazarus's life. But Jesus also points to himself and declares, "I am the resurrection and the life. Those who believe in me, even though they die, will live, and everyone who lives and believes in me will never die" (John 11:25-26). Those who believe in Jesus find life. This life is eternal life, which starts in the here and now and extends beyond the grave into eternity.

Jesus not only displays power over death but also shows that the powers of darkness are under his control by casting out demons. Jesus meets a man with an unclean spirit in the synagogue on the Sabbath (Mark 1:21-28). The demon recognizes Jesus as the Holy One of God. Jesus rebukes the demon and commands the unclean spirit to come out of the man. On another occasion, Jesus cures a blind and mute demoniac, "so that the one who had been mute could speak and see" (Matt 12:22-23). Jesus encounters still another man possessed by many demons who was living among the tombs. The man is out of control, unrestrained because of the violence of the demons (Mark 5:1-20). Jesus again shows his power over deadly demonic powers by casting them into swine.

The story of the boy with the demon whom the disciples cannot cast out highlights the faith of the boy's father (Mark 9:14-29). The demonic spirit makes the boy unable to speak and repeatedly throws him to the ground, casting him into fire or water. Jesus commands the spirit to come out of him, telling his disciples that only prayer can overcome this kind of spirit.

In another example of Jesus casting out demons, a foreigner, a Gentile woman, shows faith in Jesus (Mark 7:24-30). This mother comes to Jesus and begs him to cast out the unclean spirit from her daughter. Jesus heals the child at the entreaty of a pleading mother, and when the woman goes home, she finds the child lying in bed and the demon gone.

There are several more examples of Jesus healing those outside the Jewish community. In John's gospel, a Gentile, a royal official whose faith in Jesus causes him to go to Cana, begs Jesus to heal his son who is ill in Capernaum (John 4:46-54). When Jesus tells him to go because his son is healed, the man goes at once and finds his son healed; he and his entire household believe.

While Jesus is in Decapolis, a Gentile territory, the crowd brings a man to Jesus who can't hear or speak (Mark 7:31-37). Jesus takes the man aside—away from the crowd—and uses spittle to heal him. The healing astounds the crowd. Jesus is announcing his loving, healing, reconciling presence not only to the children of Israel but to the whole world.

In the story of the ten lepers, Jesus enters a village in a region between Samaria and Galilee (Luke 17:11-19). Ten lepers approach him and call out to him for mercy. When he sees the lepers, he tells them to show themselves to the priests. As they are going all ten lepers are cleansed, and one of them returns and falls at the feet of Jesus and thanks him. This leper was a Samaritan, who was a foreigner and neither Jew nor Gentile. When he returns to Jesus praising God and thanking him, he is showing a deep healing beyond his leprosy. He has faith in his relationship with Jesus as his savior.

Jesus heals those with longstanding diseases. Jesus heals a woman who suffers from a hemorrhage for twelve years (Mark 5:25-34). She suffered greatly at the hands of many doctors and spent all that she had. But her illness only grew worse. From the strict perspective of the law, this bleeding makes her ritually unclean and cut off from her Jewish community. She is so convinced that Jesus can heal her that she reaches out and touches the hem of his garment. Jesus doesn't become unclean because of her contact with him; rather, the woman is healed and restored to life because of her touching the clothes of Jesus.

On the Sabbath in Jerusalem, Jesus heals another man who could not walk (John 5:1-15). The man was sick for a very long time—for thirty-eight years—and Jesus tells the man to take up his pallet and walk. In John's gospel, it is this healing on the Sabbath that begins the persecution of Jesus by the religious authorities. Jesus uses this event to show that physical healing is only the beginning. There will be greater things to come. Jesus will not only heal but also raise the dead (John 5:21).

John's gospel also describes the healing of the man born blind (John 9:1-41). Jesus reaches out to this blind man. He dispels the mistaken idea that the man's blindness is a result of sin; rather, his blindness will serve as the means "that God's works might be revealed in him" (John 9:3). Jesus daubs spittle and mud on the man's eyes and tells him to wash in the waters of Siloam, and the man gradually gains his sight. The man born blind starts as someone with little knowledge of what happens to him and transforms into a person of faith, with complete certainty about Jesus' identity as the Son of Man.

There are other instances of Jesus healing blindness. He meets two blind men on the road, crying out to him for mercy (Matt 9:27-31). They affirm their faith in Jesus' ability to heal them and he touches their eyes, their eyes are opened, and they see. Likewise, blind Bartimaeus is begging by the Jericho road as Jesus draws near (Mark 10:46-52). The crowd tries to silence him, but Bartimaeus is persistent and attracts Jesus' attention. Jesus calls Bartimaeus to him and asks, "What do you want me to do for you?" (Mark 10:51). He asks Jesus to give him sight. Jesus recognizes his faith and restores his sight, and Bartimaeus follows Jesus.

Jesus reveals himself as a healer of the spirit as well as of the body. A group of four people bring a paralyzed man to Jesus (Mark 2:1-12). This time the crowds are so large that the man's friends must drop the man to Jesus through a hole in the roof. Because of their faith, Jesus forgives the man's sins and then enables the man to walk. The scribes see this healing and suppose that Jesus' claim to forgive sins is blasphemy.

The Sabbath healings—of a man with a withered hand (Mark 3:1-6), a woman who is crippled (Luke 12:10-17), and a man with dropsy (Luke 14:1-6)—also trigger the fury of religious authorities. The religious leaders' rigid interpretation of the law helps set the stage for their rivalry and conflict with Jesus, who tells them unequivocally that it is lawful to do good and to free people from bondage on the Sabbath (Mark 3:4; Luke 13:16).

And then there are times in the Scriptures where the text just says that Jesus healed those who came to him

(Mark 1:32-34; Mark 6:56). Notice there are no mass heal-ings in crowds. No huge rallies or some sort of mass hysteria. There is nothing magical about Jesus' healing. These healings have a quality of care and compassion. Notice that they're all individual. One to one to one. And they're usually seen by somebody else. The witnesses re-spond in two ways: they affirm Jesus as a divine person in the mix with God, and they recognize his healing work as ushering in the reign of God. So, there are declarations of faith, both by the witnesses and by the person healed.

We've seen that Jesus healed in the synagogue or on the Sabbath or when all else failed and the disciples couldn't do it. Sometimes Jesus healed at a distance. Sometimes Jesus healed by asking something of the person being healed: stretch out your hand or stand up and walk. Sometimes he just put mud on the eyes or touched the ears. There was a gesture. And the person healed had to receive it.

And sometimes Jesus healed without the person even asking for it. He saw the troubled widow of Nain and cured the body of her dead son. Jesus also healed simply by being present, like the woman with the hemorrhage who touched the hem of his garment and was healed. Her faith attracted the healing power of Jesus, and he felt the power go out of him.

Jesus' healings show that he is the presence of God in the world enabling humanity to live a new life. Those healed by Jesus become free to become who they are meant to be, part of a community that lives in gratitude and praise, extending God's work of restoration and healing to the world. Witnesses are astonished.

Scholars dispute the exact words that Jesus uttered. There are several versions of what he taught. But there is no ambiguity in his deeds. He went about doing good. He healed, gave comfort, and released individuals from their afflictions.

Was Jesus Angry?

Let's take a long look at Jesus driving out the money changers in the temple. The importance of this exegesis is to ask carefully whether Jesus was angry and why. If Jesus was angry and did harm intentionally, then this narrative runs counter to all episodes where Jesus supported, healed, and restored life.

Each gospel includes an account of Jesus' confrontation with the money changers in the temple. The Synoptic Gospels all place this event at the end of Jesus' ministry (Matt 21; Mark 11; and Luke 19). Although each Synoptic Gospel differs in detail, they all portray this event as the decisive moment that brings about Jesus' passion and death. The Gospel of John places this incident at the beginning of Jesus' public ministry (John 2). In John's narrative, Jesus refers to himself as the temple and says, "Destroy this temple, and in three days I will raise it up" (John 2:19), a foreshadowing of both Jesus' death and his resurrection.

So, what are we to make of this uncharacteristic outburst of Jesus? How does it square with John Cassian's rigorous teaching on anger? "Our Lord and Savior . . . desired to remove completely the 'dregs of wrath' from the innermost depths of the soul."[2] Cassian's instruction merely echoes Jesus' own uncompromising words in the Sermon on the Mount, which suggest that anger is as serious an offense as murder. Jesus says, "You have heard that it was said to those of ancient times, 'You shall not murder'; and 'whoever murders shall be liable to judgment.' But I say to you that if you are angry with a brother or sister, you will be liable to judgment" (Matt 5:21-22).

Was Jesus angry? None of the gospel accounts describe Jesus as angry. In fact, Matthew's gospel describes the chief priests and scribes as angry. The brief accounts of the cleansing of the temple in the Synoptic Gospels give so little detail that we can conceivably picture Jesus acting with composure and deliberation.

In John's gospel, Jesus makes a whip and drives out the large animals destined for slaughter. Clearly John's narrative provides a more vivid picture of Jesus' actions than do the Synoptics, a portrayal that reasonably could be interpreted as anger. But notice how he frees the birds, turns the tables, and strikes no one. He quotes Scripture texts that would have been known to the officials but harms no one.

What is the significance of Jesus' action? If we, as readers of the gospels, refrain from conjecturing about Jesus' emotional state during the cleansing of the temple, we arrive at the meaning of these revelatory texts. These pericopes seem not to be psychological texts. They are prophetic texts. This sounds simplistic, but it's hard to overemphasize this point. The point of the story, and the reason why it is in each gospel, is much deeper than to reveal Jesus' psychological state of mind. This is prophetic action: Jesus replaces the temple. There's no more need for animal sacrifice and a layer of priesthood that decides how to offer prayer. There is a new reign of God that expresses the prophetic witness of the Old Testament.

Those who saw Jesus in the temple would easily have grasped the symbolic nature of his actions. The Hebrew Scriptures show prophetic actions throughout the history of Israel. We'll look specifically at the prophets Isaiah, Jeremiah, Ezekiel, and Hosea.

Isaiah walks naked and barefoot for three years as a sign of the captivity of Egypt and Ethiopia to Assyria (Isa 20:1-6). Isaiah's action symbolizes the shame and defeat that await the two nations and serves as a warning to those in Israel who want to seek security and alliance with military strength rather than seeking security in the Lord.

Jeremiah smashes an earthenware jug to symbolize the fate of Jerusalem if the people refuse to listen to the Lord and give up their idols (Jer 19:1-15). Later, Jeremiah wears a wooden yoke that symbolizes a willingness to obey the Lord, accept defeat, and endure their exile to Babylon. During their exile, Israel will be in a better position to restore its relationship with God. In a worldly sense, the exiles have lost everything, although reliance on these things was just an illusion. Stripped of these illusions, all they have left is the reality of an intimate, restored relationship with God (Jer 27 and 28).

The Lord instructs Ezekiel to act out prophetic signs. He makes a clay map of Jerusalem and sets up a mock siege around it, warning the exiles not to hope for rescue from the doomed city. Ezekiel places an iron plate between himself and the map of the city, standing for the barrier of sin between the people and God. Ezekiel lies on his side for 430 days eating siege rations, symbolizing a people enfeebled by their sins. Ezekiel shaves his head and beard with a sword, the very military instrument used in Jerusalem's defeat, symbolizing the humiliation of defeat and loss of vanity (Ezek 4 and 5).

In the book of the prophet Hosea, marital infidelity symbolizes Israel's abandonment of the Lord. Hosea's marriage to the prostitute Gomer is a prophetic symbol of the Lord's enduring, unshakeable relationship to unfaithful Israel (Hos 3).

So, Jesus' behavior in the temple matches other prophetic actions directed toward Israel, gestures that were sometimes peculiar and perplexing to those who saw them. In all three Synoptic Gospels, Jesus accompanies his act with words from two prophetic texts: "'My house shall be called a house of prayer'; but you are making it 'a den of robbers'" (see Isa 56:7; Jer 7:11). The reference to Isaiah emphasizes the universal vocation of Israel to draw all nations to the Lord, a vocation that Israel is not living out. The quote from Jeremiah rebukes Israel for their illusion that the temple itself is enough to sustain a relationship with God. The den of robbers refers to those who seek security in outward religious activity in the temple. Israel must learn that sacrifices in the temple are meaningless without true and heartfelt devotion to God.

Matthew and Mark link the temple incident to the story of the withered fig tree, a prophetic sign of Israel's lack of spiritual fruit. This image in the gospel is a stark contrast to Israel's true calling as described in Hosea, where God compares finding Israel to the delight of finding a fig tree's first fruit (Hos 9:10). Moreover, in Matthew, Jesus heals the blind and the lame at once after driving the buyers and sellers out of the temple (Matt 20:14). And as we saw earlier, the gospels link Jesus' healing to the prophetic tradition of the Suffering Servant who comes to heal and restore the people of God (e.g., Isa 35:5-6).

How do we interpret Jesus' actions through the lens of the Old Testament, especially the prophetic tradition? We have Jesus' teaching on anger in Matthew's version of the Sermon on the Mount.[3] Jesus' actions in the temple achieve the prophetic vision of the Old Testament. In Jesus we find the purpose of the temple and all Old Testament realities. Jesus is the new temple, the new dwelling and meeting place of God. Jesus came to heal, to hold, and to bring to a close all former ways of using violence as satisfaction. No longer is it fitting to offer bloody sacrifice. His body and blood, his passion and cross, his laying down his life was the beginning of this New Reign, this New Kingdom of God. Jesus shows us the way to be for one another in this Easter time. We see Jesus' complete giving of himself in the way he endured his suffering and death on the cross. Jesus did not use violence to end violence. He could have used righteous anger for the sake of justice, but he did not react or bring force to vanquish his foes.

Jesus Renounces Violence in His Passion and Death

Each gospel tells the story of the passion and death of Jesus.[4] An innocent victim, Jesus ends humanity's horrific cycle of rivalry and violence. God's response to this iniquity is to raise Jesus from the dead. Just as Jesus showed his

authority over the powers of darkness by casting out demons, so does Jesus show his dominion over the power of
humanity's violence through his passion, death, and resurrection. The passion narratives in the gospels point to Jesus'
refusal to retaliate against the forces aligned against him.
Instead, we see Jesus having a deep understanding of the
motives and forces working against him.

As Jesus enters Jerusalem on Palm Sunday, he spoils the
expectations of those who were looking for a triumphant
messiah, a messiah who would aggressively crush anyone
who challenged him. Instead, Jesus enters Jerusalem riding
a colt, recalling Zechariah's messianic picture of a humble,
peaceful king who shuns militaristic trappings and conflict
(Zech 9:9-10).

Throughout the gospels, Jesus predicts his passion and
death. For example, in Matthew's gospel, Jesus clearly describes what will happen: "You know that after two days
the Passover is coming, and the Son of Man will be handed
over to be crucified" (Matt 26:2). Jesus understands the
events that are unfolding, and he is ready for them. He is
clear about his fate and faces it steadfastly. These dreadful
events are met with astonishing equanimity and/or appropriate measured response; he faces adversity with peace
and poise.

During the Last Supper, Jesus announces that one of his
followers is going to betray him. Again, Jesus knows exactly

what is happening, and he is in complete control. Jesus' impending death is not an accident or a scheme gone wrong: "The Son of Man goes as it is written of him" (Matt 26:24). Jesus takes no action, no retaliation against Judas. He does nothing to stop Judas from his betrayal.

After the meal, Jesus reveals that the rest of the disciples will abandon him, recalling another prophesy: "Strike the shepherd, that the sheep may be scattered" (Zech 13:7). Peter responds and rejects Jesus' declaration that he will abandon Jesus. Jesus affirms Peter's impending denial, without bitterness or indignation.

Betrayed, abandoned, and facing a cruel, violent death, in Gethsemane Jesus recoils against the unfolding events and poignantly refers to himself as sorrowful "even to death." Beyond the physical suffering that awaits him, the sadness and sorrow become unendurable as he struggles to accept the cup his Father has given. Yet Jesus is still the faithful Son, willing to complete the mission, to complete the work he has been given to do: "not what I want but what you want" (Matt 26:39).

Judas and a large crowd approach Jesus to arrest him. The crowd, armed with weapons, reveals the violence in the hearts of those who seek Jesus' death. Suddenly one of Jesus' followers draws a sword and cuts off the ear of the slave of the high priest. In Matthew's gospel Jesus vigorously rejects the violent and inept attempt to protect him (Matt

26:51-53): "Put your sword back into its place; for all who take the sword will perish by the sword" (Matt 26:52). Jesus could call on the limitless spiritual powers available to him—twelve legions of angels—and he does not. Jesus refuses to take part in the endless cycle of escalating violence.

In Luke's gospel, Jesus responds to the attack on the high priest's slave by saying, "'No more of this!' And he touched his ear and healed him" (Luke 22:51). On the brink of his own violent death, Jesus reaches out in compassion to reverse the violent act of one of his followers.

Jesus then challenges the crowd, calling attention to their weapons, and asks them why they are armed. Jesus never did anything that would make it necessary for them to arm themselves: "Have you come out with swords and clubs to arrest me as though I were a bandit? Day after day I sat in the temple teaching, and you did not arrest me. But all this has taken place, so that the scriptures of the prophets may be fulfilled" (Matt 26:55-56).

Jesus appears before Caiaphas the high priest, and he is brought before Pilate the governor by the chief priests and elders. He refuses to answer the accusations of the chief priests and elders, and this silence amazes Pilate (Matt 27:14). Pilate recognizes that Jesus is innocent (Luke 23:14-15), yet jealousy and competition for power seem to be the motives behind the religious leaders' desire to crucify Jesus (Matt 27:18). The cycle of violence intensifies. The crowd becomes agitated, insisting that Jesus must be crucified, and Pilate hands Jesus over to be flogged and crucified.

Luke's gospel depicts Jesus speaking words of forgiveness from the cross, even as the soldiers and crowd torment him: "Father, forgive them; for they do not know what they are doing" (Luke 23:34). Jesus, approaching death, proclaims forgiveness to those who are responsible.

Again in Luke's gospel one of the two thieves crucified alongside Jesus proclaims the innocence of Jesus: "We indeed have been condemned justly, for we are getting what we deserve for our deeds, but this man has done nothing wrong" (Luke 23:41). Again, with no evidence of desire for revenge, Jesus reaches out with compassion and love to the repentant thief and says, "Truly I tell you, today you will be with me in Paradise" (Luke 23:43).

Luke's gospel underscores Jesus' innocence one final time when the centurion praises God after seeing Jesus' death and says, "Certainly this man was innocent" (Luke 23:47). The crowds who see Jesus' death return home, beating their breasts (Luke 23:48). Like the centurion, they recognize the injustice of what they have seen and perhaps their own complicity in it.

The passion narratives show Jesus as an innocent victim, suffering at the hands of those who are ignorant of Jesus' true identity. We see that Jesus is the way out of violence. His incarnation, historical sacrifice, death, and resurrection reverse the cycle of violence. His commission to his disciples was to do likewise, in his name. We also see that Jesus endured violence without action of retaliation that escalates the cycle of violence.

We see that Jesus healed those who were harmed. There is no anger in Jesus, and he was not the object of the wrath of God. Jesus reversed the ritual patterns of bloody sacrifice offered at the temple of worship. Jesus reverses the scapegoat mechanism[5] and all other retaliatory reactions to violence. Jesus is a way out of violence.

Chapter Three

About How God Has No Wrath

If I could put what I believe about God in fewer than two hundred words, it would be this: Jesus is the Way for us to shift from violence to healing. Jesus has a face like mine. We are loved. Through the cross and the crucifixion, Jesus reversed all the previous victim incidents. Jesus took upon himself all violence and came out the other side. He rose from the dead and breathed on us peace. Jesus spoke and lived his historically Jewish life in relationship to his Abba/Father. As his followers, we are invited into this same loving relationship. This love is an abiding presence. We pray to God and feel God's response of holding us in love. God is praying in us, to us, too. Through Jesus, we are one, center to center. This Mystery is holding from the center of all our ambiguity, all our confusion, all our ups and downs, all our propensities. We are being held firm, safe, and secure in the grasp of the Holy Spirit. I feel that I'm just lying in that wound of Jesus' right side. There is no wrath in God, only love.

Julian of Norwich's Influence through *Lectio*

A few years ago I had the privilege of giving a retreat at the Benedictine Monastery of Stanbrook in the United Kingdom. The nuns had recently taken a bold step to shift out of a major classically built facility and relocate hours away. The old Stanbrook was near Worcester and is a two-and-a-half-hour drive or about 150 miles northwest of London and the new abbey is at Wass, a four-to-five-hour drive north of London, 250 miles. I flew into Heathrow and took the train to York, where I was met by Sister Anna and driven the hour to Stanbrook Abbey. The new building was nestled in a sweeping countryside shared with flocks of sheep and miles of woods protected by vast Yorkshire moors.

The retreat was on our common Benedictine roots as sourced in desert spirituality that influenced the Rule of Benedict. What was new to my studies was the English Benedictine mystics Gertrude Moore, Catherine Gascoigne, and Dom Augustine Baker, as well as the story itself—how the nuns' community was founded in 1633 by the English Benedictine Congregation and then exiled until after the French Revolution. They had a rich and sturdy mystical tradition of writers, artists, and musicians. I read the story of how these nuns were the conduit for the famous manuscript of Julian of Norwich, who wrote in the fourteenth century. Julian's long text of eighty-six chapters of *Revela-*

tions of Divine Love is a treasure. It was soon my text for sustained *lectio*, which has the usual four dimensions of lectio: literal voice is read by the logical mind, the symbolic voice is read by the intuitive senses, the moral voice is read by the personal senses, the mystical voice is read by the spiritual senses.

First, the literal reading, which studies the text with the logical mind.

Second, a longer, lingering delving into the insights and symbols, reading the text more like poetry with the intuitive mind. This took me a couple of years.

Then, third, I delved into the mandate of the book. Julian had a message for Meg. There emerged a moral imperative to see the good merciful Lord as Julian did. This personal encounter with Julian as a text, as a person, and as a master teacher gave me pause. There's meaning in sin and suffering now that will be revealed later. But for now, we can be comforted that God's love is ever abiding and much more than we can imagine. This moral sense I received from the revelations given to Julian sifted deeply into my Catholic soul—her circular pattern of writing about her received tradition that sin caused suffering in this lifetime and in the next. She was a loyal daughter of the church who would have been taught that sins need to be forgiven through the sacrament of confession and that there was the dread of punishment due to sin in the next life after death.

Her revelations were carefully written so that she avoided being burned at the stake as a heretic. One device she used was to be poetic and confirm the current teachings of the church. Then, she'd be subservient to say that in her particular experience she'd have no evidence of a wrathful God needing a harsh, judgmental church.

In the 1300s, there would be a list of sins that could be forgiven and one would have a happy death, but there still would be punishment due to sin that would be paid after death before entering heaven and an abiding blessed union with God in eternity. There would also be sins that would cause mortal consequences, such as being deprived of God for all eternity, and there would be punishment that would be like fires of hell for all eternity. The soul would be damned. The church was entrusted with judging the sin and mediating God's mercy so that sins would be forgiven. But all sins still had consequences after death and before heaven. The redemption from our sins was bought back through the suffering, death, and resurrection of Jesus Christ and through him we were brought to the Father fully justified. Our sins and the sins of the world were remediated and fully remediated by Jesus' sacrifice on the cross.

The church was instituted to be that medium wherein the life, death, resurrection of Jesus Christ was actually replicated for all of us. The church was the earthly representation of the holiness of Jesus to facilitate grace and mercy.

Through the church, sins were forgiven. Through the church, graces were bestowed from birth to death. The church could act in the name of Jesus and bring us all alike to the next life that held the promise of paradise, but it also had the role of being the judge and facilitator of the Last Things, including death, judgment, punishment, and salvation.

When I lingered long into the life, text, and literature of Julian, I met a strong voice that explicitly said (a) that there's no wrath in God; (b) that God loves us and sin cannot divide us from God; (c) that even the way things are now will have an end that "all will be well, all manner of things will be well, and that we will each have our own experience that all will be well."[1]

More than a feel-good saint who has made it and is sending us encouragement from afar, I felt that her text mediated the message. So which is it? Is there a tradition in the church that comes from this little-known text of the fourteenth century that is a private revelation and is scarcely known except as a footnote in the likes of Thomas Merton or a mention in T. S. Eliot's *Four Quartets*?

Or is the Catechism the real revelation that has chapters and chapters classifying sins and consequences?

Or can they both be true?

As a mortal and just one Benedictine nun who's read, studied, and lingered with the text of Julian of Norwich, but has also read, studied, lingered for fifty years with the sacred doctrines of the Roman Catholic Church, I can hold these two traditions together with the knowledge that the church has two thousand years of wisdom. Each of the sections of the Roman, American, and pastoral documents of the church is a response to a particular situation(s) that covers a vast quest to implement the mandates of the Scriptures, the teaching of the church, and the pastoral governance of baptized Catholics. The church teaches that sin is forgiven through the sacraments, yet the consequences of sin follow the dead into eternity. God's mercy prevails, but judgment is also satisfied through purgatory and/or hell.

I can do as Julian did. She remained a loyal daughter of the church. She simply raised up that she witnessed no wrath in God, only love. In this book on renouncing violence, it seems wise to embrace this loving God who does no violence to us or any creatures. Is there a risk that we would harm our souls and the souls of others if there's no punishment due to sin? Julian is simply saying that our motivation to do the right thing is also our love for God that has been planted deeply in our sensitivities. And where there are limitations, we offer those faults and failings to our merciful God. We are saved simply by being created from all eternity in the mind of God. This is the Good News!

Finally, the fourth sustained layer of *lectio* with Julian was the wonderful immersion into her mystical voice that transmits her experience to the reader. Spiritual senses awaken that receive the content. For the sake of this chapter, I will share two experiences of being at the deathbed and witnessing that there is no wrath in God after death. The dying is tough, but the moment, the instant of passing through, has all the indicators that the next life is "at peace." It is in this mystical dimension that I had the experience of time that was already but not yet. In faith, I have felt an abiding joy that, since all shall be well, it already is already now. So the "not yet" is a felt "already." The mystical voice is received by the spiritual senses that have an already felt-actual of "now." This living faith gives great comfort, especially in times of trouble and distress. Knowing that "all shall be well" has the gift of already knowing this from a deep place in the heart. It's similar to the mystical oneness that there is nothing without God.

The reader might want to know why I feel so confident that there is no wrath in God.

Here, on our fifty acres of monastery grounds we have three facilities: the monastery where some fifty or so nuns reside; the Benedict Inn where there are several rooms for guests; the St. Paul Hermitage, a retirement facility for lay, elderly residents. Each year between the monastery and the hermitage we have several deaths. It's a singular privilege to be at the side of the dying one at the time of illness and death.

Death is a Master Teacher. We have a practice of keeping vigil. We have a special book of prayers that extends our Monastic Hours for the dying with songs, psalms, prayers, Scripture readings. When I take my turn sitting with the dying, I've noticed over all these years (I entered in 1961) that there is no interest on the part of the dying to hear the teachings of the church, quotes of Scripture, or even stories of the saints and martyrs. That teachable moment has long passed. What they do seem eager to hear is the way other sisters have died. What happened? Who was there? Was it protracted and painful or was there a passage into a moment of simply being taken? They want to hear that the other side isn't that far away and that there's continuity with their preciously held faith. They want to know that there is an actual someplace else, with their loved ones and with the object of their heart's desire, with God. They want to know that they've been accepted, now and at the hour of death. They want to know that there are no more expectations. Even unfinished relationships, projects, commitments are more than enough. They want to know that now there will be an invitation from the Other Side to pass through death and that all they need to do is be ready to accept. They need to know that part of that accepting is that all the fears, anxieties, and fragments no longer separate them from all that is Good, Beautiful, and Loving. There isn't even an agenda of a final consent. Death itself makes that transaction. All is at peace, one, done, and ready. Breathing is enough and soon even that won't be necessary. There is nothing more to say, confess, receive, or become. Being has brought on the next open door of birth.

These are two stories that I can report from my own experience.

Story One

I was seventeen years old. The year was 1961, in August. My mother had received a phone call from Aunt Evelyn saying that my grandmother was dying. I'm not sure why I was the only one of the six kids who went with mom to Indianapolis that hot afternoon, but we hurried the over two-hour drive down the Old Highway 41/52 to 318 N. Rural Street. Grandmother was upstairs. Uncle Denis met us at the door. He had his white, starched Sunday shirt on. Aunt Evelyn was at her side. In less than an hour she died. Mom held her left hand, and I had her right hand. I remember praying that my energy would simply jump-start her life. She was eighty-one. In 1899, at the age of nineteen, she came from near Killala Bay, County Mayo, Ireland. Her husband, my grandfather, was born near Galway and immigrated through the Irish network. He ran a grocery store near the corner of New York and Rural streets. He died before I could remember him.

Grandmother's death was around midday. No words were spoken, except the Hail Mary. Tears. The moment was not easy. She was in pain; she could not breathe. There was the smell of hemorrhaging. There was a candle, a crucifix set from a special "home sacrament kit for the dying." It was usually stored above the steps on that shelf separating the floors, but today it was at the table near her bed. Candle lit. A crucifix was mounted with the crafted board for this very purpose.

I could always feel her hand in mine. This sealed, like being close, sort of chosen, even special. In a very odd way, her death brought me closer to her than we were in life. It's hard to explain how death is a connection. The Irish talk about "a thin place." I know both "the thinness" and "the place."

Thirty years later, at St. Francis Hospital in Beech Grove, we gathered around our mother during her last moments. She had told us that before her father died he told her to never be afraid because at her death he would come to get her. We reminded her of that offer from Grandfather Hannon. She smiled. She asked us not to touch her as she had to do this alone. Her death was being fully alert and taken. Her chestnut brown eyes seemed to those of us standing around her hospital bed to be awakened by someone.

Story Two

After Morning Prayers one Thursday morning in March, Sister Ernestine asked me, "Where is Sister Joanie?" I didn't see her in church, but had seen her the evening before, when she had phone duty at the reception desk. I went up three flights of stairs and down a long corridor to her room. The door was locked. So I went to the treasurer's office, asked for the master key, and returned to the room. On opening the room, I found Sister Joanie, lying in her bed, eyes wide open. She had a smile that was a wide, awe-struck, open-mouthed gasp of delight! The bed linens were tidy, hands folded on top. Her head was slightly flung back and her shiny-silver hair nicely posed. There was one window open about seven inches. The curtain was softly blowing. And yes, there was a delicate scent, faint-but-felt. I paused. Holding my pounding heart, I gasped, "My, my!" I left her and called in the nuns. We prayed the prayers. She was no longer with us here.

So, God has no wrath. Then, what? Judgment, punishment, eternity? Being with the dying, I can feel our mortal side of fear, anxiety, pain, and dread. Yet the death itself is kind. I've seen that the actual death is a moment in time, like stepping out of the shower. Does God receive each of us with a total loving embrace? Or are there interim stages of testing and trials?

Like Julian of Norwich, I've seen no wrath in God (Fifth Revelation). I've seen difficult dying phases but no actual death that would even hint that there is wrath on the other side. I don't believe that there are interim stages and further testing with trials to purge wickedness. We die in God's loving arms. The rest will be revealed, that is, the Good News into this New Reign of God. We can trust that the God who created us from all eternity would be that same ongoing life force through all eternity. "The now" is to trust this loving God. More than that comforting claim, I also believe that we'll know each other just as the disciples knew Jesus after his resurrection before he ascended. We will have our unique subtle bodies that are distinct persons. In the next life(s) we'll not have limitations of time, space, and place; sheer grace will be our known experience. We can trust that this is also our tradition, our commonly held faith claim.[2]

We now turn to the Gospel of John, which is our revelatory text that substantiates all the good news we've had from our own personal experience.

Chapter Four

About How God So Loves the World

We see that the passage through death leads to the other side. There's no wrathful deity snatching life but an invitation to further shores in another life. In Scripture is there a tradition of this loving God that lifts us to the other side without the peril of punishment for sin, consignment to purgatory, or hell for all eternity? Is the cycle of violence perpetuated on the other side, or is there peace and eternal well-being? Where can we find this tradition in our Scriptures? We study the Gospel of John.

Jesus comes into the house where the disciples are gathered on Easter Sunday night and says, "Peace be with you." Then Jesus breathes on them and gives them the Holy Spirit, and with the Holy Spirit comes the mission to carry out Jesus' message of God's love and forgiveness to the world. In her fine work on the resurrection texts of John's gospel, Sandra Schneiders makes a case for the following translation of John 20:23: "Whose sins you shall forgive they are forgiven to them and those [meaning the *people* whose sins have been forgiven] whom you embrace are held fast."[1] The implication of this translation directly from the Greek is that a person's sins are forgiven and, once forgiven, the church embraces and supports that person within the community and against the evils and dangers in the world.

The disciples carry on Jesus' mission of receiving those whom the Father gives them. Jesus in the flesh is no longer in the world, but they, his body, the community, are in the world (John 17:11). The disciples will do his work, even greater works than Jesus did during his earthly ministry (John 14:12). As the agent of the departed Jesus, the community does not exercise judgment, which Jesus explicitly said he was not sent to do (John 12:47). The church gives voice to faith in this "good God" who sent us this "loving Jesus" who completes creation that was God's plan of Love. As Julian of Norwich articulates so well, "The Revelation is Love."[2]

This is the real presence of Jesus: the ecclesial body, the eucharistic body, the textual body of Scripture. It is also expressed in the spiritual tradition of the mystics, where we see the direct experience of Jesus as friend, lover, and spouse. "John's gospel is a primary source and resource for the experience in the church of the glorified human Jesus personally alive, present and active throughout all time. The church's spirituality is an ongoing exploration of the existential meaning of Jesus' promise."[3]

John's gospel also proclaims the Christian revelation of God's love for the world: "For God so loved the world that he gave his only Son, so that everyone who believes in him may not perish but may have eternal life" (John 3:16). This love is manifested in action, in the coming of Jesus in the flesh, and in his death; the Greek grammar emphasizes that this is a supreme act of love.[4] This passage about God's love for the world appears during Jesus' conversation with Nicodemus, a Jewish leader who comes to Jesus at night. In John's gospel, the night symbolizes evil and ignorance. We see how Nicodemus struggles with Jesus' strange insistence that he must be born again. Jesus often uses figures or metaphors to describe himself or his message. This language often leads to misunderstanding on the part of his hearers as they struggle to shift from the earthly to the heavenly plane. We watch how Jesus insists that those who encounter him in the gospel and we ourselves must stretch our understanding of earthly things in order to attain light and life in relationship with him. As we read John's gospel, we become more familiar with the language Jesus uses and more confident in his love for us.

Jesus also demonstrates who he is in the miraculous signs he performs in the first part of the gospel: turning water into wine at Cana (John 2:1-11), healing the lame man at the pool (John 5:1-18), the miracle of the loaves (John 6:1-15), the healing of the man born blind (John

9:1-41), and the dramatic raising of Lazarus from the dead (John 11:1-44). Mary and Martha explicitly describe Lazarus as one whom Jesus loved. Jesus' love for Lazarus prompts raising Lazarus from the dead. This act will glorify God and foreshadows the resurrection of Jesus from the dead and the promise of eternal life for those who believe in him. Thus, the terror of death has been conquered. Nothing on earth claims this supreme power of merciful love.

John's gospel describes Jesus as the Son who descends from heaven to the level of humankind and then returns to heaven, bringing humanity up to the level of the divine. This cycle of coming from heaven to the world and then returning with humanity back to heaven is the arc of God's love for the world.

This is significant. If we posit a wrathful God who is disappointed in his creation then God is sent to test his creatures, even cause suffering. Can our creator God be mean-spirited? Would God exact a penalty for satisfaction? If Jesus is sent to make reparation for sin, then Jesus is a victim of God the Father's wrath. All this anger and cycle of violence justifies more punishment and vindictive violence. Justice is not served by causing harm.

Then, if indeed you extend wrath to the church, the church continues the juridical rage of God by judging and retaining sins against people in the hopes that they comply and behave better. Maybe members would be more compliant if punishment was the deterrent, but wrath seldom brings the best motivation from those who have been harmed. We know from our own lives that, when harmed, we tend to react and retaliate. The cycle of violence spins faster with more force that causes more harm. If Jesus is angry, and God is full of wrath, and the church is an instrument of punishment, we miss the Good News, the revelation of the incarnation of Jesus, and the fact that God so loved the world that he sent his only Son.

In John's gospel the story is love. God sent the Son to complete creation and bring all of us back to the original fulfillment of extravagant love. The sin of the world is the rejection of God and his son Jesus, who came into the world to manifest God's love and compassion for all of creation, for all of humanity. When Jesus returned to the disciples, even after his tragic death, he did not seek vengeance or retribution; he did not blame or punish. Jesus brought forgiveness to all.

We have a propensity toward sin. God's mercy completely overshadows[5] that human condition and does not hold it against us. We don't know the origin of sin, and even though multiple and complex theories about sin abound through the two thousand years of Christianity, we can say that, through Jesus, we are loved and held in his grasp and that we are returned to the Father already saved and loved and completely forgiven.

It is fitting for us as Christians, then, to start with ourselves and renounce violence in all its forms, thereby embracing this revelation of love. It seems that we can raise up this sturdy tradition stored in the Gospel of John, which picks up the Genesis creation motif with mystical confidence. This is the experience of early Christians, and it is our experience now. The positive experience of Jesus coming to breathe the Holy Spirit on us and living in the Spirit that he has given us provides us with the very capacity to renounce violence. We have help, an advocate, an accompaniment that gives grace for that which seems impossible by nature.[6]

I'd like to conclude this chapter by saying again that the revelation is love, that no sins are held against us, and that we are forgiven. There is no wrath in God, no anger in Jesus, and the Holy Church is established to care pastorally for us. We can count on the Holy Spirit to provide the promptings of grace as to how to renounce violence. "The glory that you have given me I have given them, so that they may be one, as we are one, I in them and you in me, that they may become completely one, so that the world may know that you have sent me and have loved them even as you have loved me" (John 17:22-23).

Yes, the Good News can shift us from harm to healing. The harsher texts about a fierce God, an angry Jesus, and a punishing church belong to an earlier tradition that need not be retrieved in our perilous times. There have always been multiple traditions living side by side in our history of religions, more specifically our Judeo-Christian heritage. We cannot afford raising up justification for violence with sacral legitimation that God was wrathful so we can continue the cycle of violence.[7]

In the next chapter we consider more about the Holy Spirit that has been sent and how this Holy Spirit is at work among us, moving us toward the peace that Jesus promised us.

Chapter Five

About the Holy Spirit and Discernment

Come, Holy Spirit, Come

Part 1: The Holy Spirit as Guide

Renouncing violence is not optional. Action must be taken. But how, when, where, and with whom to act is tricky. Reactive jerks feed the cycle of violence. Violence begets violence. Jesus came into our world and reversed all violence with his loving way of laying down his life. He breathed on us the Holy Spirit. We now continue this compassion through the directives of the Holy Spirit. We know that violence was negated by the offering of Jesus in his death. A completely innocent victim has remediated and reversed all the violence in history. This is the faith claim of Jesus' incarnation, death, and resurrection.[1]

Of ourselves, we are hardwired toward rivalry and competition, toward putting ourselves first and taking advantage of the weak and vulnerable. This is our human condition. For this book we are not examining the causes of violence or doing a theological review of traditions that trace possible insights and wisdom that ease the pain of our existential precariousness.[2] We have made the claim in chapter 2 that Jesus is the Way out of violence.

Jesus initiated the new reign of God. In him it is already completed, but we have not yet experienced the full revelation.[3] And the "not yet" part is where we participate in knowing what it is that we should do or refrain from doing. We count on the directive of the Holy Spirit that Jesus breathes on the disciples that Easter night and is given to us.

Jesus presented himself alive to the disciples with many proofs that he had suffered. Jesus appears to the disciples for forty days, speaking about the reign of God. After the ascension, the disciples gather together in Jerusalem: "When the day of Pentecost had come, they were all together in one place. And suddenly from heaven there came a sound like the rush of a violent wind, and it filled the entire house where they were sitting. Divided tongues, as of fire, appeared among them, and a tongue rested on each of them. All of them were filled with the Holy Spirit and began to speak in other languages, as the Spirit gave them ability" (Acts 2:1-4).

In this book, *Renouncing Violence*, we speak of the need to trust that the Holy Spirit has been given to all of us, not just the few who lived historically when Jesus of Nazareth was teaching and healing. We too can rely on the impulse of the Holy Spirit and follow Jesus. Given the vast studies of early proclamations after Pentecost through teachings and liturgies, I'm selecting seven characteristics of the Holy Spirit that give us confidence in this presence.

First, the Holy Spirit is the presence of Jesus in our history, just like Jesus was historically present in his lifetime. This presence of the Holy Spirit is distinctly a gift given by Jesus and it is a specifically reliable way of being Jesus in our times.

Second, this Spirit is other than ourselves and other than Jesus. We can trust this Spirit descending on us and entering our consciousness, our very way of being together as an ecclesial community. So, this Spirit enters our very lives, but it remains a distinct person. We are not left orphans. This faith claim prevents the tricky self-consciousness from taking the proper place of a God-consciousness.

This is not dualism to have the humility that I'm not God. When I was stranded for five hours on a mud relief in the Rio Roche near Cochabamba, Bolivia, I had the raw experience of nakedness and was immersed in fear that was deeper than any river. I shook to my existential core. I am a mortal creature.[4] This felt "otherness" is sweet when "held, as in the mother's womb," but it can also be a tremendous fear when existential dread becomes the "terror in the night."

Because of the human condition I cannot trust that my thoughts, my emotions, my inclinations are toward the good, toward God, or toward the benefit of others. I have strong tendencies to be self-centered and be competitive toward others. I can also trick myself into thinking that I'm better than I am, so I can take advantage of others. Sometimes I look back on my actions with regret. If I knew then what I know now, I would have behaved differently. Sometimes I notice that I act without knowing and find out later that I was wrong. Since the accident in Bolivia I have a felt experience of always being in need of God's mercy. I'm ready to repent of my wrongdoing. This gives me proper relationship with God and with others. I am not my thoughts, my emotions, my passions, and my self-constructed identity. Through God's mercy the Holy Spirit can gently prompt me toward right relationships with myself, others, God, and our cosmic and local universe. I need help. I count on God's grace.

Third, this Spirit is distinctly given, breathed on us by Jesus. This given Spirit is received, and the Spirit acts on our behalf as an advocate. With the Spirit we have a way of being in the hostile world with fortification, with strength, with God-given energies that keep us safe, keep us on message, and keep us together with confidence. The Spirit has been given, yet it is wise and helpful if we "ask" for the Spirit. To acquire the Spirit as a felt presence we invite, welcome, treasure, and behold as Mary did when visited at the Annunciation.

Fourth, this Spirit is the soul of our soul. This animator quickens our life principle and infuses us from the inside as a dimension of perichoresis: we are inside the inside, cohering. There's also the resting of God in us. There is nothing not God. All mystical is ineffable but real and distinctly felt by the spiritual senses. The spiritual senses can distinguish between oneness and distinctive otherness. Mystery!

Fifth, this Spirit is here whether we feel it or not. It has been given and is an opportunity to grasp being grasped by the revelation. This Spirit holds us together, holds me in a relationship with Jesus, who, if I see the face of Jesus, brings me into the realm of the Father, toward God. This Holy Trinity is not just a literary device but an absolute, critical way of being in a relationship with God as a human. And Jesus, with the human face, is my opportunity to pray, be understood, be known, be loved. The historical Jesus is no longer in this realm of my history. But he did not leave us orphans. He gave us the Holy Spirit. And this Holy Spirit is at work in me, in us, in all of us.

The Holy Spirit is an essential way in which we continue the realm that Jesus chartered in his earthly times. And it's the Holy Spirit that will help us shift from harming to healing. We enter this dimension in prayer. Prayer is a heartfelt, faith-filled time and space of my presence in the presence of God. We have a sense of ourselves in the presence of God and we wait upon the Lord.[5]

Along with our invitation to seek God's help there is a felt impulse that we need to invite the Holy Spirit, invoke the Holy Spirit. This is called epiclesis:[6] to call down the Holy Spirit to be present and consecrate this moment, this time, this event, and to especially create the new era. The reign of God is one of peace and empathy, compassion, understanding, wisdom, and a right relationship with God.

Sixth, Jesus is embodied in community as well as the individual soul. Ecclesial communion is the Holy Spirit continued in our midst. Jesus was deliberate in gathering his disciples as a group, a community, a sharing of the experience of being called into this new reign of God. This revelation is called church. More than a faith community of shared beliefs, this collective consciousness is embodied in organized and intentional relationships. This church has been gathered together to live the Good News of this God who loves us so much.

Finally, the Holy Spirit is identity without entity. This is difficult to put into words, but in my *lectio* about/in/with the Holy Spirit I find that our relationship with the Holy Spirit is more than the cosmic Christ, more than undifferentiated matter, more than a force field of the Holy One, more than a continuation of the presence of Jesus, more than the heart's desire toward the Abba/Father, and more than a handy patron or whisper of the "Hail Mary." This identity seems to have no entity, no line of demarcation that defines where s/he's not. So, identity without entity, a face without "other." Mystery, for sure.

I'm always surprised to hear very devout souls who make choices to do this or that without any consideration of how the Spirit might gift them with the grace of insight and right action. It's not uncommon for me to hear someone make a total vocational life change based on one's own thinking mind without any prayer, without any discernment with the Holy Spirit. How does it work if we make decisions through discernment rather than through planning with the self talking to the self?

What is deceptive is that both one's personal presence of oneself and the Presence of the Holy One are undifferentiated sensations. Both are mystery. But one has ego-driven propensities while the Presence of the Holy Spirit is compassion, meekness, and kindness. Discernment can sort out which one is of God and is to be acted on. One's own consciousness and the Presence and/or consciousness of God are never in opposition because God loves us as we are. Whenever there are harsh oppositional impulses between one's ears, that is never God. God is always loving, kind, and consoling.

Today we talk about consciousness and mindfulness. This is a dimension that gives gravity to spirituality. The Holy Spirit, however, is more than the collective consciousness or even an individual's consciousness. That's why I prefer the concept of identity without entity. The Presence of the Holy Spirit is distinct and can be felt by our spiritual senses.[7]

The experience of impulse for good toward God is called the moral voice in tradition. The experience of God at work in me intertwining my own personal actions is the mystical voice. The moral is outside motivation, and the mystical is inside motivation. Sustained discernment can bring us to this mystical place of inner stillness and then our witness, our actions are sourced in the Holy Spirit. This is often called contemplative living.

Part 2: Discernment When Faced with Violence

Discernment to Write This Book, Renouncing Violence

When I decided to write this book, it was not just one or two conversations with the publisher and then a simple decision to offer a proposal. I went into the sustained practice of discerning if this was God's preference or Meg's ambition. Discernment took intentional time and sequential steps. Discernment replaces planning. It is an encounter with the Holy Spirit. Here are the steps I took in praying through the decision to write a proposal.

Step 1: Ask the Holy Spirit for the right question. My concern was the disquiet around the 2016 presidential election. I knew I wanted some way of responding to violence that

was not going to create more violence. A working definition
of violence includes forms and forces that cause harm. With
the 2016 election, I felt there was harm to civility, to cordial
diplomacy, to honest reporting of news and events, to giving respect to those who differ in tone or in trust. As a nun
I've always been proactive toward the poor and vulnerable.
I felt that my cherished values had recently been inversed—
not only reversed, but inversed. The status quo was the
other direction of my cherished values. Given the climate of
conversations in my monastery and among family, students,
friends, I could see that divisions were deeper, wider, and
critically sensitive. It seemed to me that:

- if I joined any resistance group, it would soon be pro-
  test and not demonstration;

- if I wrote a scholarly paper on a topic like climate
  change, it would be countered and/or dismissed;

- if I organized or joined a dialogue group in process
  with my former colleagues of East-West Dialogue,
  we'd be talking to ourselves;

- if I did symbolic action, such as fasting or a marathon
  of prayer, it would not be noticed and just pile up
  vainglory for myself;

- if I participated in social media and wrote more letters
  to editors and gave voice to opposition, I'd just feed
  talk about the talk;

- if I organized a meeting and convened folks on current topics, I'd just repeat my pattern of overwork, fatigue, and sickness;

- if I did research on climate, immigration, health care, and/or disparity between the rich and the poor, no one would read it, and someone would write the opposite message with other statistics and alternative persuasive arguments;

- if I remained passive, the void would shout louder; aggression is like liquid finding a way to leak and seldom is it smart to go into freefall; for me, anger rises and judgment diminishes,

It seemed to me that what I've done before and could do again was write a book that would be read and would contribute to a deeper conversation sourced in my received tradition. A book might contribute to significant further insights. So, I asked the Holy Spirit to clarify for me what is the right question: "Do You want me to write a book? and on the topic of renouncing violence? Is this the right question?" I asked respectfully and with indifference about the answer.

I heard in my prayer, "Yes."

Step 2: Watch and sort thoughts. I made a virtual decision on one side or the other of the question. "Yes, write a book" was my virtual decision.

Now I began to watch thoughts rising. I took note of the ones from God, from self, from others, or from evil. I watched not only the source but the direction: toward God, toward others, toward self, toward evil.

Here are some thoughts that rose: "I'm smart so I can put out on paper compelling reasons to renounce violence"; this is from a self-centered source. "It would be good for my prayer to do *lectio* on the gospels and see how Jesus managed violence in his historical life"; this is from God. "I have readers of the Matter series. Those same readers might benefit from this too"; this is from others. "I could use the book writing as an excuse to drop out of the rigor of the common life here at the monastery"; this is from evil.

I sorted thoughts for a week or so, until there seemed to be strong support for a yes to write the book. Sort and watch what the motive is for writing it. Is it helpful to others? And is it something blessed by God?

Step 3: Make a tentative decision. Come, Holy Spirit, come. Yes, I'll write a book on renouncing violence. But I need a confirming sign that this is not coming from my ego-driven tendency.

So, I asked for a confirming sign from the Holy Spirit. The sign should be big enough to consider the matter at hand: writing a book. The sign should pertain to the decision at hand. It should be from the outside and not conjured up by my imagination. The sign should be firm and not unsteady, hot one minute and cold the next. Finally, the sign should give confidence to decide and implement without hesitation; this is the actual grace.

I was amazed at not just one confirming sign, but five. First, resources came my way both for skillful assistance in writing this manuscript and to pay for a computer upgrade. Second, the outline for the book was already in my head, and I did not need further research. It just needed to be written. Third, the holy water ministry was already in process. I have been giving holy water bottles to those who are receptive. Toddy Daly, my friend and collaborator since the 1970s, when we worked for the archdiocese, and with whom I worked for the Monastic Interreligious Dialogue Board in the 1980s, found that holy water created zones of peace that calmed fear and anxiety. I just needed to write a catechetical piece on the tradition of holy water.

Fourth, I was inspired by Pope Francis's encyclical, *Laudato Sì*, which calls us to care for the Earth. His whole text is about renouncing violence. We are invited to change our lifestyle and regard creation as sacred.

Finally, I felt an invitation to write this book differently than previous books. I was invited to write this book with poise and patience. I was invited to practice renouncing violence in the writing of this book. Specifically, this meant that I was to refrain from straining my eyes and skipping meals, sleep, or common life.

Step 4: Make the decision. I wrote the proposal to Liturgical Press. I received permission from my superior. I signed a contract.

Step 5: Guard the heart and watch thoughts. I watched for thoughts that take away either the decision, the discerned motivation, or the discipline to do the work of implementing the decision. The decision was made after prayer and discernment. I could embrace the project with confidence in God's grace.

Note that making decisions through discernment is prayer rather than planning. The point is to notice the thoughts rising and observe. Look at all thoughts and sort into buckets. Notice if the God bucket is filling up. It's good to take at least a week for this part of the process so that there's time for the mind to bring to one's attention all aspects. Also notice that discerning isn't thinking; rather, it's the observing mind. See the thought as a unit from the outside and not analysis or going up the train of thought that has a life of its own. You are looking at the question, noticing the thoughts rising, and seeking God's will. What does God want?

Discernment is a process to determine what decision is to be made firm and what action needs to follow. Let's review the steps of discernment that lead to action and changing the forms and forces that cause harm:

First, we pray. We ask God to direct us to just what is the right question at hand. What is the matter that needs a discerned response?

Second, we take the "given" question and the optimal outcome. This is in our mind. We virtually use our thinking mind to come down on one side of the question with a preferred outcome that would be a decision.

We take time to observe our thoughts. We sort them into buckets of thoughts from the good, thoughts from God, thoughts from others, and thoughts that are bad. We take days and maybe even weeks to do this sorting. We watch how the thoughts are giving signals as to what we should do.

Third, if the thoughts stack up on the side of "good" or God, we make a tentative decision to answer the virtual question and make a decision. But we refrain from acting on the decision until we have a confirming sign from the Holy Spirit. This should pertain to the matter at hand, be from the outside, and be positive, accompanied by joy and some grace to implement the decision, even if it is difficult. Should there be no confirming sign and thoughts of confusion and ambiguity, we go back up the process and ask again if this is the right question and the right side of the action that needs to be taken.

Fourth, we make the decision and ritualize it in some form. Send an email, write a letter, do the first step of the decision.

Fifth, then, once the decision is made through prayer and the practice of watching and sorting thoughts, we hold fast to its outcome and resist the temptation to undo the decision.

Taking Action

Renouncing violence leads to action that heals harm and prevents suffering. Our faith is of two kinds: one aspect of faith is "that which" we believe. Chapter 2 is about Jesus, what we believe about Jesus. It is an example of that kind of faith. The second aspect is that "by which" we believe and that "by which" we act into our faith and be the Christ for others in our midst. Renouncing violence has a major obligation to change the forms and forces that cause violence. The example of writing this book is the second kind of faith "by which" we take action and use our faith as energy and strength.

It is acutely difficult to respond to violence in a way that refrains from reaction, causing either subtly or blatantly more violence.[8] The Holy Spirit is our advocate, so we can take refuge in the Soul of our soul. Sometimes, however, we can't hear that still, small voice because of our destructive emotions. The next chapter is my own story of a protracted bout with the affliction of anger.

Chapter Six

About Anger

As we saw in chapter 2, Jesus reversed the cycle of violence. We examined the actions of Jesus healing harm, doing symbolic action to usher in the reign of God, ending the ancient temple sacrifice. We also saw that Jesus endured suffering rather than reacting with righteous anger during his passion and death. Our faith teaches us that just as Jesus harbored no anger, reversed the victim-atonement-redemption cycle, so can we. There is no wrath in God. The church is the pastoral continuity of the reign of God in ongoing revelation during our times.

Violence begets violence. Renouncing violence is the only way to get on the other side of the afflictive emotions and find the peace we desire. Jesus breathed the Holy Spirit on us and this Uncreated Energy we call God is at work in and around us. Through the Holy Spirit we can discern what action we should take in the face of whatever force or form violence takes. When our consciousness is covered in anger or another one of the afflictions, we can't hear, feel, or know the Holy Spirit. This chapter is a teaching on anger. Anger, my foe, became my friend, but only after years of inner prayer and ascetical work. Thanks to the mercy of God!

A Dispute with the Chaplain

Several years ago, when I was prioress of my monastic community, I had a dispute with our community's chaplain.[1] The archbishop appointed this priest to provide liturgical services reserved for an ordained clergyman. I observed troubling events that prompted me, as superior, to believe he wasn't helping us but rather was not a good fit for our community. I wanted him replaced.

"We need another chaplain," I told the archbishop. He said, "You just might get somebody worse, or no priest at all."

I went to my council of advisors within my community. They said, "He's good enough. He gets along with the rest of us."

I fussed and fumed. My displeasure with the chaplain continued to bloom into a full affliction of anger. It appeared I could do nothing. I had to go to Mass like all the other nuns and listen to him, but no one listened to me, the superior. He also had a residence on our monastery grounds. He got a stipend, a house, all the services provided by our community of about one hundred nuns at the time. My anger swelled into a full fog over my consciousness. I was long past the tipping point of a working relationship without inner resistance.

I'm not sure what the turning point was, but one day I asked our Lord: if I couldn't get rid of the chaplain, would our Lord help rid me of my anger? Every day for three or four months I went to the monastery's oratory where there hangs a large crucifix. The oratory is an intimate space with room enough for about eight nuns to sit in the presence of the crucified Christ. Each day, and sometimes a few times a day, I would sit there. I would lay my angry thoughts at the feet of our crucified Lord.

At first, I would pour out my tears of frustration. I wasn't contrite. I was right. I wasn't soft-hearted or converted or reconciled to the fact that I could not relieve myself of this chaplain whom I felt interfered with my way of praying in church. I still attended the Masses where he was the presider, but I still wanted him replaced with a chaplain I thought more suitable for my community. I felt no compassion for the man; I felt only my hard heart. I continued to put that anger with point-by-point detail at the feet of Jesus. I continued to ask God to remove that anger. As awful as it felt to me to encounter this chaplain every day, it was worse carrying around this heavy, cold, hard heart. So, I had, in effect, two problems: the chaplain and my anger.

When I sat before the crucifix in the oratory, whatever angry thoughts or feelings came, I lifted them up and mentally placed them at the feet of Jesus. You probably can guess the outcome. First, I began to feel a certain ease. It carried over into the liturgies which were officiated by the chaplain. There was ease too in my consciousness. Walking from here to there, I no longer obsessed with the thought of this chaplain. Then I experienced a shift in mood whenever I would sit at Jesus' feet. I would be present and nothing—no thoughts at all, certainly no angry thoughts—would be there. It was just me at the feet of our Lord. I imagined myself somewhat like the woman at the banquet who poured her tears and the ointment on Jesus' feet and dried it with her hair (Luke 7:36-50). Of course, it wasn't quite that dramatic, because I merely sat there, dwelling in Jesus—just sitting there, time and time again, at the feet of Jesus. The sitting was the prayer.

After about a year, the entire affliction passed. By the grace of God my anger moved past that glaring conscious stage of alert rage against the chaplain. He remained with our community for years beyond my terms as prioress. In those post-leadership years, I was able to reach out to him. He was battling cancer and received my full support and that of the community during some grueling years of treatments both here in Indianapolis and in Chicago. In his final days, he lived in his home monastery. When I visited him, I felt only compassion for this man struggling with a terrible illness. A few months later, I attended the funeral that celebrated his life. My foe became my friend.

My anger affliction also became my teacher. My dispute with the chaplain wasn't the biggest problem I faced in my time as prioress. My anger was. My attachment to my own righteousness was formidable. It created a steady stream of wrath and sarcasm that radiated around me. Living in this state of rage was destructive mainly to me. The most serious damage was that it produced a very hard heart. I lacked compassion toward the chaplain, who, in the time my anger was directed at him, was in the early stages of cancer. My anger was more dangerous to me than if I had cancer. Anger was ingesting me, eating away all the light in my eyes.

Something else happened too during my hours before the cross. By the grace of God and the prompting of the Holy Spirit, I encountered the first stage of conversion. I realized that the situation was out of my control and power. As long as I was carrying this affliction, I was going in the wrong direction and taking my community with me. So there was a *metanoia*. There was a change of thinking. And there was the recognition that I needed help. I wanted our Lord to lift this affliction from me because it was harmful to others and to me. The one thing all people with addictions realize is that you can't get on the other side of addiction by your own efforts. You need help. I needed help.

The harm to me was that I could not pray. The directive of the Holy Spirit saved me: I was to take this affliction and lay it at Jesus' feet. The affliction was my prayer. I lifted up my hard heart to God.

The ongoing process is to listen to the prompting of grace. In my case, I found a prayer form, sitting in front of our Lord Jesus crucified on the cross, where I could lay out my heart. The way out of this affliction was a grace. Earlier in my journey, I perhaps would have thought that some aspirational prayer would relieve my suffering. But I needed grace, and I also needed to sit there every day and be humble at the feet of Jesus, to bow my head and kiss those feet, and to put my hand in his side, asking for help. I needed this personal gesture as well as formal prayer, which I continued to do with community: Liturgy of the Hours, Mass, and other gatherings.

Also, I realized that just going to confession would not ease the grip of this affliction, either. Once, during one of our community penance services, I was tempted to go to confession to this chaplain, but as I was walking toward his confessional I pivoted to another priest because I realized I was going to use confession to let him have a piece of my mind!

My affliction didn't ease quickly. It needed long, pleading prayer—even at the point when my mind became conscious of the change I wanted in my heart. It took a long time to move that anger out of my heart, out of my body, out of every cell that was infected with the intoxication of self-righteousness, the scourging thought was that I was so right and everyone else so wrong. This disease, this virus, this absolute infection of anger didn't move out suddenly. It took time. And it moved out in surprising ways. I never had a moment of conversion during my sitting in the oratory or at the common prayers in chapel. My affliction of anger moved out gradually and in various places—while I walked or drove a car or wrote my correspondence and did the other work of daily life. In other words, rooting out an affliction of anger takes time, it takes form, and it takes a steady practice.

This isn't merely a question of resolve. I refrained from resolutions because I knew they wouldn't do it. They would serve only as measurements of my failure to live up to my own resolve. It took kind of a natural, organic pattern of letting go and moving on, because my desire was to not be angry. I saw that anger was an obstacle to my prayer, my relationships, my service, and the well-being of my body. Anger causes anxiety and agitation. When I'm perturbed, I react more quickly to triggers because I can transfer that anger instantly to somebody else. It's a learned response that prowls about, seeking whom it may devour, as the Psalmist says in Psalm 91:5-7. It is the terror of the night, or the arrow that flies by day, or the pestilence that stalks in darkness, or the destruction that wastes at noonday. My adversary was like a roaring lion, walking about seeking someone to devour (1 Pet 5:8).

The experience of my anger with our chaplain and how that affliction eventually left me after lingering at the feet of our Lord showed me how I can change behaviors I no longer want. It was, in one sense, quite a gentle transformation. And yet, my anger was extirpated, literally pulled up by the roots. It is a grace available to all of us who suffer an affliction of anger.

Notice also why this story of anger is chapter 6 in this book: We saw in chapters 2 and 4 that Jesus reversed the victim-atonement-redemption phenomenon. We did careful analysis of Jesus' symbolic action in the temple. Jesus had no anger. The emotional state of Jesus is not the subject of the content in Scripture. Jesus harbored no anger, even during his passion and dying on the cross. There is no wrath in God. The church is the pastoral continuity of the reign of God in ongoing revelation during our times.

In the early monastic tradition, "right effort" is to do the inner work of renouncing anger; then God springs up. God is there all the time, but an affliction like anger places a dense fog in our consciousness. When the anger was lifted, I was naturally meek and kind. I did not have to practice being kind to the chaplain. The affliction shifted like the weather; the storm passed. On the other side of anger, I did not need a reconciliation with this chaplain; I simply could relate naturally and with appropriate emotions. He received my change of heart graciously.

You might ask if my affliction of anger returned from time to time over these years. The answer is yes, but it was not as protracted or as stubborn. Chapter 7 gives some detail about how to prevent and to move out afflictions before they become such full-blown passions.

Chapter Seven

About the Practice of Renouncing Violence

My anger dissipated. Without anger clouding my eyes and ears, I could see and listen to the nuns in my community. As prioress, I had an opportunity to learn the Rule of Benedict from a new and deeper perspective because I taught a Holy Rule class every Wednesday afternoon at four o'clock. To my surprise, the theory behind Benedict's Rule is the training of the mind. While I had prayed for relief of my anger I received a gift beyond gifts. I found the foundational theory behind the monastic way of life. The chaplain remained, but I discovered that anger was a learned response to adversity and that I could also unlearn it. I found in the early writings of the monastic tradition a sturdy teaching that was "practice," a training of the mind that dealt with any and all afflictions. The classic afflictions are around food, sex, things, anger, dejection, acedia, vainglory, and pride.

Earlier in this book we saw that there is no anger in Jesus, no wrath in God, and that the Holy Spirit provides every grace necessary. We saw that we are hardwired toward violence[1] and need to undergo a thorough training to renounce our own tendencies. If we react without discernment, we tend to contribute to the cycle of violence rather than shift harm to healing. See the select bibliography to go deeper and find resources on the classic training of the mind that is universal, no matter which spiritual path one takes toward one's heart's desire.[2] In this chapter, we'll go through a summary of teachings from that early monastic tradition.[3]

The training of the monastic way of life has an inner goal: shifting from self-consciousness to an immersion into a mystical consciousness, a knowing and experience of God acting from within, rather than the self acting toward self. This prevents untamed instincts from prevailing and promotes God's reign. This shift is to have the self in service of God rather than God in service of the self.

Part 1: Shifting from Self-Consciousness to God-Consciousness

Question: How can someone like me, in my normal life and routine, put renouncing violence into practice?

Response: Let's start by defining a few concepts:

- The working definition of violence: forms and forces that cause harm

- The working definition of practice: training of the mind that changes self-consciousness to God-consciousness

The mind can unlearn destructive emotions and tune the heart to listen to the Holy Spirit. We can imitate Jesus through the grace of the Holy Spirit. By training the mind, we can get to the other side of our afflictions and shift our self-centered ego-consciousness to a God-consciousness. It seems that little children have this natural affinity toward God, but as we mature, self-consciousness becomes dominant. We can return to this original innocence through training of the mind to lay aside self-consciousness.

Question: It seems that "training the mind" is key. What do you mean by training the mind? Is it even possible? How?

Response: When I was in Tibet and India, Buddhist monks and nuns hosted us. They undergo extensive training of the mind. We, the Benedictine monastics, realized that we were highly trained into the content of our Catholic faith but had little or no training of the mind that directs the process of the thinking mind. Along with Buddhist and Hindu monastics, we Christians soon learned that we can redirect our thoughts, our motivations, and our emotions. Our thinking mind as a verb rather than a noun leads to right actions. So, we train our mind's eye away from self-centered, self-driven ego-consciousness toward seeking God-consciousness in our mind's eye.

The first step is to watch our thoughts. To watch them is to notice not only the content of thoughts that loop around and ultimately cause unwanted actions but also the stage of the thought, to catch it early, even to anticipate its rising. This attention offsets what formerly was working on the mind unconsciously. If we are vigilant, we can anticipate situations or catch the first inkling of thoughts that get us into trouble. We learn to notice afflictions rising—no matter what the content (food, sex, things, anger, dejection, acedia, vainglory, and pride). We can train our mind away from the content of the thinking to the process of the thinking mind that leads to virtuous action. We have a specific way to root out afflictions so we can hear the impulse of the Holy Spirit.

You can gently but quickly use these practices to root out the affliction. The five antidotes are:

1. Pray without ceasing by using a mantra.

2. At the first trace of temptation, pray an arrow prayer like, "O God, come to my assistance. O Lord, make haste to help me."

3. Shift your attention from the afflictive thought or emotion toward selfless service or another prayer practice, for example, the Little Way or the Practice of the Jesus Prayer.

4. Remember your death.

5. Combat the affliction with a quote from Scripture.[4]

All of these antidotes require watching and observing our thoughts. Watching thoughts presumes we know the anatomy of a thought. We watch how these thoughts rise, and we use one of the antidotes to refrain from being engaged with the thought and consent to its harmful invitation.

Question: What about this anatomy of a thought? Could you elaborate?

Response: Let's run through a realistic sequence. Note that the sequence is the same for a good action as well as for a destructive action. If the thought is harmful, it's a vice; if the thought is helpful, it's a virtue. For the sake of this teaching let's assume the thought is toward harm rather than toward the good.

- A thought rises, an image appears.

- The image is accompanied by self-dialogue.

- This extends to mental action, such as continuing the dialogue as emotions rise.

- I consent to the inner promptings of further images and conversation inside my head, accompanied by feelings.

- The thought gets solid and becomes an entity, offering a suggestion to take action.

- I either act or refrain from the invitation/temptation.

- I act on the invitation this time.

- I continue in the direction of the original prompting (an affliction).

- I continue being engaged with that thought that is now an entity with emotion (passion).

- I act often in collaboration with the entity, and it becomes a habit (pattern).

- I then dwell in that ethos of suffering (pathos) until
  . . .

- This entity becomes my identity (captivity).

- I mistakenly believe that "I am the thoughts."

Observe with the mind's eye how the "I" wants to control. Counter this by training your thoughts to shift into discernment when reacting emotionally. Some examples are as follows: pray to Jesus, our Lord, who has a face like ours. Renounce harsh self-talk. Rely on the Holy Spirit for what, when, how, and to whom we resist violence. Refrain from judging others. Renounce guilt and allow mercy to be received. Forget harm done. Cultivate a ceaseless default prayer practice, for example, "Jesus, mercy!"

Question: I thought we were talking about experiencing God-consciousness, about attaining rather than cancelling. How does experiencing God-consciousness fit?

Response: This is a perceptive question. You're right. Training the mind is more than backing out of the afflictions. There is also the positive work of cultivating God-consciousness. Prayer replaces food-consciousness, sex-consciousness, thing-consciousness, anger-consciousness, and so on. Prayer cultivates a God-consciousness.

Yet, there's another tradition that is side by side. There seems to be a both/and effect: on the one hand, we back out our afflictive thought and cultivate a virtuous thought, but on the other hand, there's another tradition that is laced right between the lines of these sturdy teachings. This other tradition simply says that when we lay aside our afflictive thought, the Spirit simply springs up. Given that the Soul of our soul is the Holy Spirit, we can feel the surge of the Spirit when our own self-consciousness relaxes and steps aside. This simple consenting to the lifting out and away of our afflictive thought is our right effort. The Holy Spirit does the rest. There's something quite peace-filled about not needing to do the additional work of supplying the virtue. We wait upon the Spirit. All is gift. We accept grace. Again, my anger toward the chaplain was lifted. I did not cultivate meekness; it came naturally. When the anger lifted, I felt the presence of the Holy Spirit instead of my anger, rage, and steady state of self-righteousness. This is a delicate distinction that has a both/and answer: We lift out the afflictive thought, wait for the Spirit to fill with grace (even though it is also a grace to have the impulse to lift out the afflictive thoughts), then, in the waiting upon the Spirit to fill our hearts with grace, we accept the new impulses toward charity and meekness. Grace abounds.

In all humility, we cannot do this by our own effort alone: (a) repent, change our minds; (b) await the grace to fill our hearts; and (c) act on the new grace received. What seems contrary to the subtle movements by the Spirit is to (a) declare our competence to make these amends and (b) to construct virtue that roots out our vices. All of this is grace, and we accompany the subtle invitations of grace with the supple willingness on our part. This can't be taught, only caught. With experience, this is obvious, but from the outside and maybe by judging ourselves or others harshly, there are great gaps that prevent this anointing and bestowing of grace upon grace.

Question: Can't I just want my ordinary prayer to lift my burdens?

Response: This working with the thoughts is the training of the mind. Wanting prayer to do the work is aspirational rather than ascetical. From the early monastic tradition, we learn how to do this inner work for the sake of the contemplative journey.[5] This is the work of renouncing violence. It's good to bring to conscious attention one's complicity and then, through training, unthink the violent reactions. In the poise and checking of the stages of the thought, we redirect our emotions rather than be victims of our emotions. You've caught the main teaching that is renouncing violence.

Question: So, is violence my problem? I thought violence was something done to me? What do I do about all the violence that comes from the outside? So far, you're teaching me that violence is from the inside.

Response: No matter the source of violence, it requires a personal response.[6] Your confrontation with violence determines whether the violence escalates or diminishes. Training your mind enables you to detect the source of violence and refrain from reacting without discrimination. To prevent yourself from being the source of violence you must keep vigilant and refuse easy entry to violent thoughts. Once one is at peace, you can hear the Holy Spirit's response and receive the actual grace to respond with decisive action.

Question: So, this book is about me? I'm the one renouncing violence? I thought I was just the one who was supposed to do something about it? I didn't cause it in the first place. Am I expected to accept the blame for violence?

Response: Blame? No. But connected? Yes. The question is what you can do in the face of violence, whether you caused it or not. The human condition is complex.

Question: Shouldn't I determine first who's to blame so I can do the right thing?

Response: Blame leads to harsh judgments and usually is not helpful. The question is how to change the harm into healing. It's hard work, whether it's done by myself or working with others.

Question: So, what is this work?

Response: Most of the time this is gradual ascetical work. We can never discount the possibility of a God encounter that zaps conversion in an instant at any time and any place, but because of our human condition we simply cannot "will it" and expect prayer to sustain us. We must do the ascetical work. We are invited do the inner work to remove obstacles so that prayer can spring up. We shift out of self-consciousness when we do the inner work to turn toward God and away from self-driven tendencies toward our ego-self.

Question: Again, why is it my work? Why isn't it someone else's problem?

Response: If you go back to the example in chapter 6 of my dispute with the chaplain it didn't matter who was right and who was wrong. I could only do something about myself. I separated out my response to the dispute and with God's grace could change. Then, I could see clearly what action to take. Simply put, an angry person becomes part of the problem, not the solution.

Question: You spoke of two traditions, one being lifting afflictions and then following the impulse of the Holy Spirit, the other of replacing the vice with virtue. I went to a Jesuit school and the emphasis there was to perform the virtues. I'll name them if you want the list.

Response: This Ignatian tradition is the dominant school of spiritual direction today. It has centuries of practice and saintly results. The church has flourished because there are many schools of spirituality: Dominican, Carmelite, Franciscan to name a few. The Jesuit influence has been the largest movement in the last five hundred years. The tradition of my vocation has been monastic, which had its beginnings a thousand years earlier in the tradition. All the charisms are skillful means to God. Mine just happens to be the monastic tradition that is sourced in Benedict's Rule from the sixth century. The monastic tradition has more emphasis on *lectio divina* and the ascetical work of refraining from afflictions rather than practicing virtues.

Question: Isn't the ascetical life rather self-centered? Practicing the virtues helps me do charitable works like you point out in chapter 2, the way Jesus lived, by healing those who have been harmed.

Response: Again, a perceptive question. The authentic spiritual paths seek God. In God, there's the mandate to love one another. It's not optional to serve the poor and vulnerable.

Question: Can't my outreach to the poor also be my ascetical work? Do I need to be so concerned about my thoughts?

Response: You've just asked me why I wrote the *Matters* series! Neither in my novitiate nor in my academic studies was I taught the theory and practice of the mind. When I was "sent on mission" as a catechist in the church I had the apostolic mandate and worked in the vineyard of the Archdiocese of Indianapolis, but I did not have training in purifying my motivations, my intentions. When I succeeded, I was at risk of vainglory, and when I failed, I was plunged into dejection that leads to depression. My inner life needed purification so that I worked on behalf of others rather than for self-gain.

Question: So, you recommend the monastic spirituality? Is it better because it's older? What about contemporary improvements in theories of the inner psychological development?

Response: I recommend the foundational training of the mind. One theory of it is found in this early monastic tradition, which can be adapted to all spiritualities. Older isn't the criteria for better, but it's a good starting point. Yet, the first study ought to be Scripture; then one is prepared for the teachings from the desert tradition. Originally, the meaning of active and contemplative life was both sides of inner training of the mind: the active life was a positive training to pray; the contemplative life was a conscious effort to back out thoughts of negative emotions (the eight afflictions).

Both active and contemplative life were ways of the spiritual journey. Only later did the active life take on the meaning of one doing outward acts of charity and the contemplative life (inner) become acts of interior prayer and ascetical work with one's inner passions. In the loss of these distinctions, there was an overemphasis on good works without interior training as to motivations with virtuous intentions, and actual vocations were split into active and contemplative. This caused overemphasis on contemplative prayer and fasting without accountability for good works and explicit social responsibility for others, especially the poor and vulnerable. This is tricky. So many times in history and even in our times religion fosters abuse rather than holiness.

Shall we go further into those teachings?

Part 2: More Theory on the Thoughts from the Tradition

Question: There is a lot of material here. Seems like if I were a teacher I'd need to know more, but I'm simply a practitioner.

Response: One needs enough theory to stay faithful to one's practice. You can judge for yourself how much conceptual background is enough. Here is a short summary of some theory, with technical language to get a feel for its rigor. Do be patient here, as the language comes from our early Greek influence. I have found it helpful, but if it deters you, know that God has ways to the soul without speculative thought.

Question: Do give me a taste of these teachings.

Response: Directors, most of the time abbots or abbesses in a monastic setting, differentiate between moments of temptation. There is the *prosbolë* (suggestion in thought), which is free from blame (*anaitios*). Next follows the *syndiasmos* (coupling), an inner dialogue with the suggestion (temptation), then *palë* or struggle against it, which may end with victory or with consent (*synkatathesis*), actual sin. When repeated, such acts produce a *pathos* (passion) properly speaking and, in the end, a terrible *aichmalosia*, a "captivity of the soul," which is no longer able to shake the yoke of the Evil One.

The proper object of *exagoreusis tön logismön* (revelation of thoughts) is the first stage of this process, the *prosbolë*. One must crush the serpent's head as soon as it appears. All of this is done through an entire strategy: *nepsis* (vigilance), watchfulness, the guarding of the heart (*custodia cordis*) and of the mind, prayer, especially the invocation of the name of Jesus, and so forth.

The theory is that our thoughts loop around and hook us. We can watch our thoughts (*nepsis*) and see the points of contact, invitation, and consent of the will. Some thoughts are slicker and more insidious and catch us before we catch them. We need help. It's good to speak our thoughts to a director who can:

1. receive our thoughts/urges

2. give us the opportunity for honesty and truth bearing

3. help us notice when we get hooked and take action that is against our best self

4. help us to notice the content of the thought (e.g., food, sex, things, etc.) and the stage of the thought (the consent, the patterns of *pathos*)

Question: That is helpful but a lot to take in. I'm struggling to find a way to wrap my head around it. This is not what I've been taught about confession. This is something different. Is there a way to summarize it?

Response: This teaching is about discernment. Through the Holy Spirit we receive the actual grace to change. Earlier in this book I wrote that evil flourishes when the center doesn't hold. Another way of understanding the Holy Spirit is to say that the Spirit is the Center. Let me offer a few intuitive concepts *we can* hold together:

- We can hear and heed the promptings of the Holy Spirit, even though we are hardwired toward violence.

- We can relax this hardwired propensity through the training described above.

- We can train toward poise and peace.

Part 3: Renouncing Violence toward Ourselves Trains Us to Refrain from Violence toward Others

Question: Can we be violent to ourselves, cause violence to ourselves? If so, what are the ways we do this, and what are ways to renounce those modes of self-violence?

Response: From early childhood, I've had excellent training on how to work. What I had to learn on my own without mentors, professors, superiors, and bosses is how to rest, how to not do. This is a key step in being nonviolent with yourself, in being kind to your body, mind, and soul. We learn how to rest, to become at home with resting. What helped me the most was not meditation practice as that seemed to perk me up and even create hyper-mental functioning. Nor was it a given that physical exercise would gentle me into a resting zone. Both meditation and physical workouts can even contribute to addictive patterns. What helped me the most is a structured renunciation, a specific intentional time for "gentling down."

First, observing the Sabbath.[7] This weekly day of rest is in our Judeo-Christian tradition. Here's a teaching on the Sabbath. I admit that my teaching is ahead of my practice, but I'm grateful for this tradition: *Keep holy the Sabbath*.

It seems straightforward: resting on the seventh day is mandatory. Our Creator God must have known our tendency to regard work as a god and to disregard the opportunity to rest. But just what is the Sabbath anyway? We learn from the Jewish mystics that there is an invisible dimension to reality that is beyond our ordinary senses of sight, smell, touch, hearing, and taste. This "beyond the ordinary" feel of daily toil and obligations is the invitation of the Sabbath. Not only is it restful, nourishing, and healing, but it is also the realm of God's intervention in our times, spaces, and places. Why is it so difficult to celebrate God-in-our-midst? The unseen, the quest of seeking meaning and significance is at our door. It's called the Sabbath.

To observe the Sabbath, it seems to me, is to recover that deepest attainment of freedom from slavery to all that keeps us busy, no matter if it is inner or outer. The Sabbath is a "together" time where we celebrate rituals and provide boundaries of space and time to nurture, not only our collective individual souls, but also our common-core being. This expands the practice from self nonviolence to community nonviolence. Making the Sabbath holy is an opportunity to step out of our working shoes—and even out of our Sunday dress shoes.[8] It is a time to sit, stand, kneel. A holy time to walk or lie down beside the restful waters of God's presence. This mind-set can also apply to opportunities like desert days, retreats, Holy Week, and so on.

A second practice is to learn to rest, to take a vocation "week in place." I get permission to "check in" instead of "check out" as we do when we leave the monastery. I post a note telling my community that I'm doing a Solitude Week in place, so I'll drop out of the common life for the designated week. It's for the sake of the common life to step back and then to plunge forward again with renewed zeal. I've had weeks at our retreat house in the woods of Brown County in southern Indiana. It's a refreshing time away and does renew and reset my soul, but this Solitude Week in place is a special treat. I do it about once a year. I call it a vocation rather than vacation because it's to "get back in stride" about my vocation. A vacation is a time away from ordinary demands of vocation.

I don't consider this a retreat that is designated time for more prayer, solitude, silence, and stillness. During the first couple of days, I take more sleep. I clean out my email and clear off my desk. If I can't do it in a couple days, I put a designated day on my calendar to get that job done. I get my hair cut, mend clothes, or finish laundry. I sort some clothes out to the swap shop, clothes I did not wear when the season was in progress. They are not doing anyone any good hanging in my closet. In the middle of the week I clean out my cell with a deliberate thoroughness. If I need something from a store, I sign out a car and go get it or do whatever deferred job that I neglected. The whole idea is to get to zero. I awake during the night. Get a cup of decaf coffee and drink slowly in a dim light. I listen to the rain, the wind against my window, and the tick of my radio clock in my cell. I purge things that cause psychological noise. Put books in library. Give away music that I'll never play because it's beyond my skillset or no longer my interest. Move on from former ways of life. Anything that pertains to my previous obligations, I don't need to keep on my radar. There's a refreshing completion to know it's over, done, and gone. It's wholesome to forget some details and *opprobria* (Benedict's word for hard work that costs sweat equity). I'm as done as I'll be during this lifetime.

Prayer happens, rises, and is never not, but during this week in place I don't fast or do extra holy hours before the Blessed Sacrament or walk an extra mile or two. This week in place is simple rest, renouncing self-violence. It's taken me a few extra years not to squander a week in place with one more project! Again, I don't consider this a vacation. Like most people I know, vacation is someplace else. This is *same place, in place, in space, in time*—just me alone with no appointments and obligations of the common life. Rest matters! Most people can't rest at home because there is too much unfinished business. This week in place does all that deferred personal maintenance.

Question: If I can't take a week in place, what else do you recommend? How can we practice nonviolence with our bodies? How can we put our bodies in good form and make them a temple for the Holy Spirit's action?

Response: We need to treat our bodies as a temple. It is important to respect our bodies and be gentle toward ourselves. Hold our body in respectful self-regard. We can start by getting appropriate sleep, accepting health, age, stage, residence, and work agreements without self-argument. We need to prevent virtual reality from eclipsing our actual way of living. It helps to measure talk, conversations, and body language to export kindness. Eating mindful of the middle way: not too much or little, not too often or infrequent, not too high or too meager in nutritional value. Plan for schedule crises and have a margin of time, heartspace, and resources to be of service to others. Enjoy body posture that strives for alignment and natural rest. Exercise appropriately. Get help for compulsive conditions that provoke anxiety and interfere with ordinary work and relationships. Accept being part of the human condition, which causes suffering.

Create zones of peace that comes from the presence of God:

- Refrain from exposing your mind to images of violence.

- Gentle down emotionally before and after stressors.

- Sleep enough.

- Do *lectio divina* on the healing pericopes of Jesus.

- Doubt harsh voices, whether heard in the head or with ears.

- Meditate, as in formal sitting prayer.

- Manage pain without suffering.

- Selflessly do manual labor (renounce doing the work for expectations of praise nor doing the work in such a way as to fear blame).

- Pray for those in need with diligent faith that prayers will be heard and answered.

- Pray for relief of one's own afflictions.

- Renounce inclinations, propensities, and addictions that diminish attention to intention and consciousness of one's own actions. If our addictions are getting in the way of right relationships and right work, then the usual treatment facilities, intervention, support groups are necessary. If addictions are manageable with ordinary good habits, do the intense prayer to the Holy Spirit and follow the pace of grace.

• Gentle down compulsions. There is wisdom in a life of renunciation. This is a preventive action. We take a vow of *conversatio*[9] in the monastic way of life. It means that we see our inner work as the work of the monastery. It's inner work that no one sees, but it's where the mind's eye stays focused, and where the mind's "I" lives.

Question: Are there ways to protect our hearts so they can stay open to the grace of the Holy Spirit?

Response: It is important to guard the heart, to prevent entrance into one's heart the persons, places, and things that take one away from God. This is an opportunity to change habits of conversation, reading, social media, interaction with others who have similar compulsions or addictions, food, entertainment, drugs or alcohol, relationships, excessive use of things, and excessive things-to-do. These all dull one's senses. Fatigue causes laxity of willingness to stay consistent to my inner disciplines. Fatigue can also cause rigidity so that there's just no capacity to have a margin of error.

So, the practice is to prevent temptation. To keep the heart pure, we practice staying in places that do not endanger our soul. The praxis is to descend our minds into our hearts and live from inside our bodies. This is advanced with proficiency in the Jesus Prayer or another ceaseless prayer.

There's so much power in prayer. The healing of our afflictions often happens. This healing literally takes away the need for managing afflictions. In chapter 6 my anger was literally no longer operational. It was gone, extirpated. It's easier to manage temptations when they are not there!

Part 4: Sin and Reconciliation

Question: Can you give us some explicit ways to live in the now while we seem to be under the burden of a culture of violence?

Response: Let's visit the sacrament of reconciliation. God, through a priest, gives absolution. This prayer is profound. Sins are not only forgiven but also absolved. This means the sins are taken away from the person's record before God. There are many mistaken teachings about punishment due to sin. Most of these teachings were meant to give the sinner confidence in God's mercy, but instead they were literal pictures of hellfire and damnation. In the healing stories of Jesus in the gospels, he simply said to go in peace and sin no more! When I teach this, I say that not only are we absolved but we are acquitted. Our sin is taken away. The church—through the priest's words of absolution—officially declares that we are not going to be punished even though we might be guilty of the charge. Our past is expunged. It is as if we did not do it. We are free of the obligation that our sins deserve. God removes our sin (and guilt) as far away as east is from west. This is good news! With this acquittal, we can start over with full energy and grace toward God and the good.

Our tradition has total trust that Jesus has reversed violence through his death and resurrection. We are now reconciled. This total acquittal differs from karma theories of the East, which posit that each of us is to pay with many lifetimes. We are free of sin because Christ Jesus took all of it upon himself. This is grace upon grace and the Good News. We are to have faith, repent, and believe in the Gospel and share this good news.

We, for our part, still feel inclined to make amends and do so not out of guilt but out of justice and right order. Making amends is also a good retraining of the habits that caused our sinful acts in the first place. Sometimes our amend is more symbolic than actual. We might contribute to a charity or do outreach to the elderly or the poor to signal our conversion.

We also pray for God's healing of any parts of us still feeling the effects of sin. We pray for the gift of compunction. This remorse is helpful to prevent sin. We even ask for the gift of tears to soften our hard hearts. Compunction is a feeling of sorrow. We pray and cultivate the abiding sense of being in need of God's mercy.[10] We long for God and feel our distance at the same time. We have an intense sense of God's loving presence. This living into the mercy of God is called *penthos*.

Ceaseless repentance is a practice. We must do our part in crying out for God's mercy. This is an amazing grace. When we have the practice of ceaseless repentance, we do not sin because we do not go up the chain of temptation that causes sin. Instead, we ceaselessly recite the Jesus Prayer: Lord, Jesus Christ, Son of the living God, have mercy on me, a sinner. The person, now reconciled with God, learns the training of the mind to prevent repetition of sin and roots out sinful inclinations.

Question: Doesn't this perpetuate guilt and shame? Seems like this would make me feel bad about myself, as in self-loathing.

Response: I can see that these teachings are too immersed into the God-consciousness zone. Your self-consciousness propensity longs for satisfaction into worthiness and refuge from your self-loathing tendencies. Remember that the goal of the inner journey is to transform that self-consciousness that has the self-talking-to-the-self into a shared consciousness with/in/through God. This mystical consciousness is a felt-faith knowing and known by God. This God-consciousness is realized in one's personal experience. Then, God acts from within rather than from without. But, this is the long, long spiritual journey.

Question: What if I have doubts in God's compassion toward my sin, toward my nonreconciliation, and that of others? Even the word "sin" makes me feel uneasy.

Response: The measurement of God's compassion, our degree of reconciliation, or the other person's willingness to reconcile are not our domain but are entrusted to God's mercy. The mystery of the "why of sin and suffering" is not available to us now. We are in the grasp of God's love. We can live with and accept doubt. The experience of humility begins to feel right. We, God willing, can train for compassion and root out hostilities in these ways:

We can cherish distinctions.

Differences need not divide.

Evil does not conquer.

Violence begets violence, so force is a last option and seldom the solution.

Extremes meet.

Unacceptable risk causes harm.

Sin, as in degree and kind, is a grid, a conceptual abstraction, a speculation. Only God knows absolute truths.

Anger is a learned response. It can be backed out. We can respond with compassion.

Religion that uses violence or abuse is not God's word or the Word of God. Suffering can be reduced when we face pain and endure what is.

Denial of the human condition perpetuates the cycle of violence.

In summary: All will be well, all manner of things will be well, and we will have our own experience that all will be well.

Part 5: Spiritual Direction

Question: Where can I get further help in training my mind, in preparation for confession of sin, in renouncing violence?
Response: Spiritual directors offer assistance for those seeking the inner journey. There is a vast array of methods as well as certified directors from many differing spiritualities. The early monastic tradition is my source in the Matters series. I have confidence in these three doors that seem to invite seekers into a deeper relationship with God.

First, there's the sustained practice of *lectio divina. Lectio divina* is a way of praying that uses the revelatory texts of Scripture, nature, or experience. This encounter with God is to listen with the ear of your heart. *Lectio divina* is our burning bush. We take off our sandals and bow our brow to the ground of our being. We invoke the Holy Spirit to bring to mind our particular text to use for *lectio divina* in the coming months. We linger with this text for months or until another text rises from underneath our consciousness. We listen to the literal voice and study with our logical minds. We meditate on the symbolic voice with our intuitive minds. We heed the moral voice with our personal senses of prayer and ascetical practices. We live the inner voice through our daily decisions and through the discipline of discernment. We receive the mystical voice with our spiritual senses. Each of these voices is distinct and is mediated through the revelatory text.

Our part in this encounter is to listen, meditate, heed with discrimination, and receive. This way of personal prayer becomes our way of life, a culture of God-consciousness. This method depends on the Holy Spirit enlightening our minds and filling our hearts with desire. The text is given to us as individuals, and we take the necessary days, weeks, and months to live into the revelation. This is sustained *lectio*. *Lectio divina* is an encounter with the living God within our loving hearts. This is our individual practice that prepares us for liturgy, selfless service, community life, friendships, and an ecclesial way of being in the world. Study skills, artistic appreciation, training of the mind for discipline, and a disposition of repentance prepare us for the deepest experience of the revelation of God. Discernment, listening with the ear of the heart, becomes a way of life.[11]

I prefer this ongoing way of spiritual direction, not just as the way I listen to others, but for my own director to hear an update of my sustained *lectio*. It's a holy conversation when someone listens with the ear of her heart to layers and layers of depths revealed in a text. This text usually has months and months of revelatory pockets of going from light to light. To do this kind of *lectio* is a way to celebrate ordinary time. I know for myself how satisfying it is to shift out of crisis where there's some big decisions to make and then glide along this sustained *lectio* for some years. The reason I feel that sustained *lectio* is the deepest form of spiritual direction is because the heart is heard. This incarnational event is the gift of *lectio divina*.

Second, there's the entry level of spiritual direction, of renouncing one's dominant affliction. A new person who comes to the monastery seeking spiritual direction is usually troubled by some stubborn event, mood, and/or one of the eight afflictions: food, sex, things, anger, dejection, acedia, vainglory, or pride. One need not have all the afflictions. It's a grace to find the door that can eventually welcome the antidote. As you read in chapter 6, I needed to have my anger diminished before I could return to wholesome relationships with God, self, and others.[12] Usually after a year or so, this kind of spiritual direction in response to crisis is replaced by sustained *lectio*.[13]

Often one learns how to deal with afflictions through one single formative event. If one is grasped by grace, then there's the energy to change and repent. The tools then become an ongoing way of life. The appropriate prayer tool seems to be bestowed rather than chosen. There's grace upon grace, for example, when one develops the habit of ceaseless prayer. The role of the director is to check in with the student and be attentive to his or her afflictive patterns and shift into the ongoing usage of the ascetical tools. Practice cannot be learned except by practice. What has been difficult for me, using this method of spiritual direction, is the few available practitioners who can help another practitioner. There's not another way to learn a practice except by doing it. The theory of a practice isn't enough to either motivate or comprehend the inner movements that happen. Only meditators can teach meditation practice. Only those who do ceaseless prayer can teach ceaseless prayer.

Third, there's the ongoing training and practice of discernment. This is making choices through the decision process of prayer with/in/to the Holy Spirit.[14] From time to time there's a crisis, as in no going back, and choices must be made. These moments are infused with the Holy Spirit, should the person be inclined to ask. Discernment is asking the Holy Spirit to make known the way and to provide the actual grace to proceed in that Godward direction. These crisis moments are precious opportunities for spiritual direction. Usually I listen and guide the person to articulate, know, and make choices appropriate for their vocation. A decision sets up a sturdy good fit that is usually right in front of their nose! Other times spiritual direction is to accompany, to linger long at the side of someone facing his or her limitations.[15] Some of these choices have deep pain and loss, but on the other side I've only seen a peace and a poise to step into their new way of life and away from their former way of life. The ongoing direction is to assist the progress of the consequences and blessings of their new way of life and to prevent a return to their former way of life. This ongoing conversion is a delicate dance in this fast-paced world with complexity heretofore unknown. Here's where the spiritual director is a lifelong partner on the journey. The story continues and the sacred choices become sweeter over time.

To renounce violence one would engage in discernment. Note that writing this book, or any initiative that involves other participants, requires personal and communal discernment. Spiritual direction would be someone listening to the stages, the process, and the outcomes of decisions made through discernment.

Question: This sounds like a lifetime of work. Does it have to be so daunting?
Response: It's a gentle invitation. Your inquiry is a grace.

Question: Where do I start?

Response: If you can manage all the arrangements, I recommend that you start with that week in place. This would give you time to get up to zero with your things, space, and place. In the light of good order, you can see what your next step is.

Question: I would need more than a week.

Response: All you need is to get started. A week is plenty of time to confront some patterns and initiate the reverse, from chaos to order. Your external environment will repattern your brain. Then, you'll be fit to begin training of the mind. Thoughts matter!

Question: Is this week in place practicing renunciation?

Response: Yes, you are renouncing violence. You are taking time to rest. Hermits do this as a way of life. We can start with good order of things. One week will reduce the clutter in your everyday life and you'll see the next step. We are all beginners.

We conclude this chapter with the gratitude for the desert spirituality of late antiquity that gives us these sturdy teachings. We now look toward a practice that bundles our faith into one traditional gesture: holy water.

Chapter Eight

About Holy Water

Part 1: The Received Tradition

We conclude this book with an invitation to use holy water. The book began with the invitation to renunciation. We learn to renounce all that is not toward God. We live the life offered to us. We call this vocation. We find our good fit, and, through gifts given, we live our life intentionally. We follow Jesus' radical reversal of shifting harm to healing. We follow Jesus who healed the sick and brokenhearted. We learn his teachings and are gathered together by him and receive the Holy Spirit. Jesus gives us his peace.

Now we turn to the observance of holy water. An observance is a practice that others can see, that others can watch us doing. This received tradition goes so far back as our collective memory can reach. We can trace its widespread usage from earliest times.

You might ask, just what is holy water? As the tradition comes down to us, there is a three-part sequence:

1. Ordinary water is fetched. In older rites of the blessing of the water, there is a blessing of salt and a sprinkling of salt, asking God to purify the water so that it can become holy water used for blessings, exorcisms, purifications, and rituals of initiation.

2. Then the ordained minister makes the sign of the cross over the holy water and reads the prayers that are handed down in the Roman Missal and/or the Book of Blessings compiled by the church and approved by the Vatican.[1]

3. Finally, the purified and blessed water is used on the persons, places, or things that we intend to sanctify.

So, holy water is ordinary water set apart and blessed, then used by the faithful to effect what it signifies, to bring the sacred into the ordinary. The traditional gesture for using holy water is to dip the finger in the blessed water and make the sign of the cross by touching your forehead, breast, and each shoulder as you pray, "In the name of the Father and the Son and the Holy Spirit. Amen."

Holy water is used for the Rite of Baptism. The newborn or the adult catechumen is either immersed or undergoes a ritual pouring of blessed water on the forehead. The celebrant speaks the solemn prayers, and all the witnesses respond with a firm "Amen." Each time holy water is used, a ritual miniature occurs of the historic immersions in the sacred Jordan River, where John baptized with water.

Holy water is a domestic sacramental used before sleep, at special events, and in blessing new cars, homes, things, spaces, places, times, and persons. Through Jesus we take up the cross and reverse violence. There is nothing that is not holy.

Holy water is used as a prayer for protection. Though we know through faith that evil ultimately is vanquished, our "now" has many zones of danger. We need that "out of time" zone of peace that protects, guides, holds fast those of us living these "in-between" times. Holy water creates, celebrates, and constitutes a zone of peace. We use holy water as a real substance to ride our faith through space, place, and time. Beyond our little gesture, we are asking God to sanctify this place, person, space, time, or even an interior trouble or bliss.

Holy water is used in all forms of exorcisms. Exorcisms are prayers, rituals, and liturgical components to "cut out" or excise evil in all its manifestations, intentions, and stored negativity. The church ordains all priests to be able to bestow the rite of exorcism, but each one needs explicit permission from the bishop to perform the ritual of exorcism in the name of the church. Nevertheless, all the faithful can use holy water with the intent to ward off evil and to invoke the name of Jesus, because Christ has overcome evil.

Part 2: Deliver Us from Evil

In this book we explore how to take the positive steps of blessing rather than be at risk for reactions to violence that serve only to harden, quicken, and widen the cycles of violence. Holy water reverses this tendency toward retaliation, fear, anxiety, and rage. We bless instead of curse. More than anything we can do, we call down God to do the work of purifying and sustaining and to deal with the evil wherever it is found.

As I studied the doctrines that address the themes of vengeance, atonement, sacrifice, redemption, and satisfaction, I discovered that these issues are intended to be ways for us to call for God's intervention. The apocalyptic literature usually portrays foes who will be punished and justice that will be done. Over the years we got the message that justice will be done but missed the part that creatures often stoke the cycle of violence rather than settle disputes. The original intent was to leave justice to God, who will prevail over one's foes. This makes the practice of holy water even more urgent. We use holy water to invoke God to overcome the evils of our times.

Evil and Satan must not be given undue attention. Jesus reversed evil, and there is no essential evil in God. Any attribution of evil to God prevents us from trusting God wholeheartedly. Genuine evil touches relationships and events, but we are wise to be very sparing in the use of the word "evil."

Evil is insidious. The more we try to define evil and face it, the more fascinating it becomes, and the more we turn it into the object of our fascination. Any of us can see this when we see someone become fixated on an enemy or rival and then, without realizing it, become more and more like the rival until they are mirror images of each other. The other side of fascination or fixation can also be an obsession with a "good" that condemns anyone who hinders ways of achieving the good. Persecution in the name of God stokes the cycle of violence.

On the other hand, if we deny that evil exists, then it slips below consciousness. This gives it power to control and cause negative consequences. The real force in the universe is love, not evil. Love seeks to rescue us from our tendency to enclose ourselves in ever-smaller spaces through fear and instead brings us into a flourishing aliveness.[2]

From the other side we will see the "why" of sin and suffering. But even now, we are confident in faith that all will be well, all manner of things will be well, and we will have our own experience of that well-ness. This faith, that there is meaning and significance, can give us the lift we need now for our spiritual journey. We do not have to figure it out. It will be revealed later. Since the thought of evil is harmful to our minds, it is better to combat evil with a gesture that embodies our faith that God is good and that Jesus has already overcome evil in all its manifestations. This gesture is holy water.

Part 3: Examples for Use of Holy Water

The tradition of using holy water is a prayer form that embodies the beliefs that we hold in common: that through the cross of Jesus the reign of God is at hand and God is with us. Here are some specific examples of how holy water can be used:

- Tuck in a child before sleep, sprinkle water around the bed, take some water on the finger and bless the child, saying a prayer, "God bless you and give you a gentle night and a sweet dream," or "In the name of the Father, the Son, and Holy Spirit." Or nothing needs to be said at all; the gesture is symbolic and carries the intention wordlessly.

- Sprinkle a new car, house, pet, or bike with holy water. Simply ask God for safety, peace, and well-being.

- Sprinkle holy water around the bed of a sick child, grandparent, or friend of the family. Bless the infirm one on the forehead. Pray for their healing and peace.

- At a family gathering, give each person their own bottle of holy water. Bless each other and pray for blessings until the next time you gather again.

- After having heard a person's story of sorrow or grief holy water is given as a gesture of being received. Ask God to heal those wounds from the inside and give them comfort and peace. Give them a bottle of holy water to continue the prayer in their household.

- Use holy water at the end of a retreat, a significant meeting at work, the end of a school year, or at the conclusion of a project at work. Bless each person with a sprinkling of holy water and an invitation to take this zone of peace with them. Give each person a bottle of holy water.

You may be wondering where you can obtain holy water. Do you need to find a monastery or a parish church? Does it have to be blessed by an ordained priest? Do you have to be Catholic? Can you make holy water yourself and simply ask God to bless it?

Holy water is available in every Catholic parish church, every monastery, and every convent. Holy water bottles are usually provided in a Catholic setting. If not, you can ask the priest at the church for assistance.

Here at Our Lady of Grace Monastery we have a large bowl of holy water in the narthex (gathering space). We welcome guests to come pray with us. When appropriate we give small holy water bottles for them to take home. It is part of our outreach in hospitality to have them depart with holy water, a zone of peace.

One doesn't have to be Catholic or even a theist to use holy water and send forth the intention that healing overcomes harm, that peace pervades distress, and that calm replaces fear and anxiety. One can bless one's own holy water and use it for a prayer, but it's a shared strength when we join the lineage by using water blessed by an ordained priest.

God hears our prayers and we can pray personally any time, in any place. Yet this holy water practice is a received tradition. This means that we did not invent it and that it comes to us through the faith and faithful usage of those who have gone before us. There's a strong satisfaction in belonging to something bigger than oneself. We are invoking a whole stream of water, not just the few drops in my little holy water bottle.

The use of holy water probably has diminished over the years because there is hesitancy on the part of the church to feed magical thinking. The holy water has no power in and of itself. It is merely a means to give symbol, gesture, and form to faith. We know we are heard, but we also know that it's not for us to determine what, when, and how God will manifest grace in our lifetimes.

This ancient practice of using holy water is available to each one of us who dips our fingers into these blessed waters. This prayer is both personal and communal. The ritual embodies our renouncing violence. The Creator God calms chaos; the Son initiates the reign of God through healing all harm; the Spirit dwells and holds us center to center. We are held in Love.

While making the sign of the cross we say:

Father, Son, and Spirit,
Through these sacred waters
Calm, heal, and hold,
Now and forever.
Amen.

Appendix One

Holy Water Prayer

As a catechist the gesture of using Holy Water is difficult to put into a teaching. Sometimes I've just shared one or several of these verse texts. Each one carry the meaning of holy water. These are a few examples that have come to mind over the years. (Sister Meg)

What one says using holy water

Bless me,
Abba/Father, Son, and Holy Spirit,
    Believe in Presence
    Know healing
    Feel quickening
    Sense Love

Bless me,
    Immersed in waters
    That purify

That protect
That perfect
That eject
   All that is not of God

Bless me,
   To sin not
   To remember death
   To remain calm
   To be at peace

Bless me,
   To prevent fear
   To calm anxiety
   To check aggression
   To pause with poise

Bless me,
   Touching this holy water
   To my head
   To my shoulders
   To my heart
   To bow
      Brow to ground

Bless us,
   We offer prayers
   For those in need

For those forgotten
For those forced poor
For life not yet lived

Bless us,

Mindful of God's mercy
Knowing

no wrath in God

no anger in Jesus

no separation from God

no separation from others

Knowing

absolved of sin

acquitted

Known

before born

Bless us,

Already, but not yet
All will be well
All manner of things will be well
Will have our own experience that all will be well

Bless us,

With the wintry, wild winds of coldness
With wet, dormant stirrings thaw
With sun-drenched pathways beckoning

With falling leaves dancing
With dawn to dusking
With creatures creating
With breeze breathing

Bless us,
To know each other
Or is it
None other
Than the One

Blessed are we,
Watered, fed, foiled
Unwired patterns
Ignorance diminished
Glory becomes
Strange integers

Blessed are we,
Shriven
Yet, hard of heart
Toward those forgiven
Why, so driven?

Blessed are we,
With holy waters sprinkle
Bedroom into sleep

Kitchen into altar
Car into safety
House into home

Blessed are we,
    As holy water
            negates evil
            hushes harshness
            holds vigil
            restores domains

Blessed are we,
    Hearts heard
    Pain received
    Hurts held
    Tears, made holy

Blessed are we,
    Sick cured
    Dying cared
    Dead remembered
    Coming ones welcomed

Blessed are we,
    Cosmos spinning
    Black holes whirling
    Galaxies churning

Micros thinning
Wonder winning

Blessed are the ones for whom
Storms, fires, earthquakes, floods
Tornados, cyclones, typhoons, tsunamis
Scarcity, drought, war, ice, and snow
All brought low and
Faith, first responder.

Blessed are the ones,
Who know water, air, and ground
Our sharing profound.

Blessed are the ones,
Who've crossed over
Birth, a narrow passage
Death, a cold await
Yet, into Eternal Gate
Grace, Grace, Grace

Appendix Two

Prayers in Time of Trouble

Deep suffering often has no words, but shared prayers are comforting. Sometimes it's better to not retell the story again as that retraumatizes rather than soothes the wound. (Sister Meg)

During Suffering

I cry.
Receive these tears.
Return my breath to softer, even rhythm.
Receive my grief.
Hold the story
Relieve the details
From sharp cutting edges
To round little bits
That have just enough
Sense of knowing.

Jesus
Of the Living Water,
Wash, cover, hover
Close over all till it's over
Swim with the tide
Shore up ground under my feet
Remove dirt from between toes
Between foes and those rows
Thorned hedges with no path
To wiggle through, glide, guide
Confide me to your wounded side.

A Prayer during Extreme Suffering

Good Shepherd,
I've been snatched
Separated, stolen,
I've been had
Though now hidden
Hallowed out
Broken.

Is it too late
For you to find me?
Is it too far
For you to fetch me?

Is it too near
For me to be seen?
Is it too much to ask
That I'd be spared
Into safekeeping?

Do I have to die too
Like you did
In laying down your life?

Do I have to wait,
Wonder, and hope
That good wins
Beauty prevails
Truth over fate?

Is there life
After death
Meaning in suffering
Love into Mystery
Matching my
Longing, while trying?

Can this little lamb
Be carried, held,
Hold up while fleeing

Or is there
No refuge
No one, no place, no face?

Is the Shepherd's
Voice that faint
Whispering tone
Droning
Desires rising
Where nothing
Else matters more
Than the "yes"
Of you.
Are we already
     Out the Gate?

Appendix Three

What I've Learned from Those Who've Been Harmed by Violence

We are accustomed to story upon story of those who have been the object of violence. New revelations dominate the pages and posts of social media. Having written the book *Thoughts Matter* now some twenty years ago, I've listened to many who come to the monastery for retreat. They confide their experiences of the afflictions of food, sex, things, anger, dejection, acedia, vainglory, and pride. Some participants come to these retreats from abroad. Some of them have received, and a few of them are using, compensation from the adjudicated settlements from sexual abuse legal entanglements. Their souls have been bruised. The most stunning report from them is that these little ones who have been so seriously harmed not only are healing but have found their soul's abiding presence. It seems to me that they've come in the back door to the contemplative way of life.

It has been a privileged moment for me to hear not just their pain and suffering but their newly found strength and courage to go on with their lives. While these stories cannot be clustered into themes or causes and effects, I've found the following spiritual jewels that emerge from their experience. We can all benefit from their wisdom.

- About the powerful: There's a good side effect of no longer being able to trust authority, those roles of power. Power surges as a defense in reaction to weakness; when there is a power vacuum, there is a tendency for domination. Power is an illusion. Those in authority should never be indiscriminately trusted. It's a hard lesson to learn, but once realized there's the solid truth and ground under one's feet.

- About the turmoil of feelings: There's confusion that causes distortion of proper emotions. Intimacy becomes a stinging force. Friendship enslaved. On the other side of separating from a harmful relationship, there is a newly found clarity, a rare purity of feeling ever-virgin.

- Innocence is the attraction: The cause of abuse is not always what it seems. The predator is addicted to innocence. They can get sex and thrills someplace else. Only innocence satisfies. Or does it stimulate the addict to need more?

- About being abused: There is a tough resilience that gets sharper with self-possessed resolve. No training is necessary to find one's core response. It cannot be snuffed out by anybody or anything.

- About death: Like Jesus says of himself, no one can take my life. I lay it down and offer it up. God shows up and saves. Violence is no match for those who do not fear death.

- About existential loneliness: It is a river each one of us must cross. We must do it alone. No partner or community can accompany one on this journey. The travel has this sequence: I am, so the "I am not" must be left behind. I feel lonely, but that's only a phase. I face God as my Creator and bow low with my made-out-of-nothing clay creature-ness. I swim toward God, *as if* I'm all by myself. I renounce all the illusions of any help as this is the one thing I must do alone because of my existence. Autonomy matters. On the other side, I find that I'm not alone. The seeking of God has a profound finding. Everyone I know is here with me.

- About reconciliation: There's no capacity to forgive and yet there's a grace that, through God, I've already forgotten the details and God's mercy prevails.

- About the way forward: Sometimes the suffering endures for years; for others there's a surge of grace that counters a fully charged remission of pain. No matter the drag that emerges from time to time, there seems to be a way forward with or without help from others.

- About the degree of suffering: The closer the relationship, like father or mother, priest or superior, the greater the degree of suffering and loss of well-being. The younger the abused person is, the more each cell remembers.

- About no solution: Sometimes this loss cannot be fixed. Living with the truth helps more than trying to "get over it." I'm free knowing that it's good enough. I don't have to try harder.

- About acceptance: It's hard enough to manage one's own anger. It's brutal to manage other people's wrath.

- About the wounded healer: Those who suffer do not necessarily qualify to help others. The wounded are not called to be the healers just because they've suffered. The only credential qualifying one to be a healer is humility.

- About being in grief: The grieved do well to take care to shift out of trauma by taking more rest and comfort in knowing it's okay to let others be first responders. There are many ways to help others.

- About the empathy deficit: Compassion is a gift that can't be acquired through training. We know the vacant stare of someone who doesn't sense how someone else feels.

- About separating out: It's good to take distance as soon as possible. This staying away is called integrity.

- About fear and trembling: Fear can be healthy. Maybe it's too risky to be driving in rain, sleet, and snow. Perhaps fear prevents trembling.

- About good guilt: Remorse is a gift, rarely given. Self-pity is being "had" twice. The first assault is enough to bear; the second wave can be avoided by rooting out the memory and replacing it with prayer or selfless service.

- About the perfect storm: The cycle of violence has its own momentum. It thrives in ignorance. Secrets extend its grasp. Mixing traces of good with lots of bad is an ancient alchemy that produces hard and fixed metals that don't melt under fire. Solution comes when bondage is irrevocably broken.

- About violence sponsored through religion: Sometimes religion needs to be renounced, at least for a time.

- About cultural sin: Systems that perpetuate violence harm the many. Most of the time, implosion causes collapse from within, but we can't wait, stand by, and do nothing. Discerned action must be taken.

- About courage: Even death has no fear for those who have known it in life.

- About rescuers: Helpers help in proportion to their humility.

- About the cost of abuse: The wounding of one is afflicting the whole. The triangle of victim, victimizer, and rescuer needs to be replaced with calming, healing, and holding, Father, Son, and Holy Spirit.

- About the resilient soul: I've found a deep down, bright place that is known only by me. It's my most stilled point of poise. When I first discovered its hollow ground I thought it was a fleeting glance of promise, but soon I could remember the scent and go there at will. It is never not. This inner stillness goes beneath chaos and has a home that seems to be there all the time. I've got something precious inside. No talking to anyone down there as it feels that it's already been said. I'm not alone or afraid. Sometimes I awake in the night and remember that I've been in my soul for most of my life. It's beautiful.

What I've learned from the stories is that the details are a sacred trust. Those who have been harmed know from experience that innocence is no match for the forces and forms that cause harm. We need God.

Notes

Preface

1. In my years of dialogue with the Intermonastic Dialogue Board, I had firsthand experience of "encounters." An example was the first Gethsemani Encounter in 1996, where we hosted Buddhists from many traditions. An encounter is a meeting in which both parties are changed in the process. There's a before and an after moment. *Lectio divina* is similar, insofar as the text encountered changes the reader and it seems as though the text is a living stream that is also ever changing. See *Transforming Suffering: Reflections on Finding Peace in Troubled Times*, ed. Donald W. Mitchell and James Wiseman (New York: Doubleday, 2003).

2. See Mary Margaret Funk, *Into the Depths: A Journey of Loss and Vocation* (New York: Lantern Books, 2011), 90–91.

3. This prayer is in the form of a sutra: "The simplest meaning of the word sutra is 'thread.' A sutra is, so to speak, the bare thread of an exposition, the absolute minimum that is necessary to hold together, unadorned by a single 'bead' of elaboration. Only essential words are used. Often, there is no complete sentence structure. There was a good reason for this method. Sutras were composed at a period when there were no books. The entire work had to be memorized, and so it had to be expressed as tersely as possible." See Swami Prabhavandanda, *Patanjali Yoga Sutras* (Ramakrishna Vedanta Centre, 1991).

Chapter 1

1. Benedict of Nursia, *RB 1980: The Rule of St. Benedict in Latin and English*, ed. Timothy Fry (Collegeville, MN: Liturgical Press, 1980), 231–33.

Chapter 2

1. Although many of the healings in the gospels have parallels, especially in the Synoptics, only one reference appears here. For more detail, see Andrew Dauton-Fear, *Healing in the Early Church: The Church's Ministry of Healing and Exorcism from the First to the Fifth Century*, Studies in Christian History and Thought (Eugene, OR: Wipf and Stock Publishers, 2009).

2. John Cassian, *The Conferences*, trans. Boniface Ramsey (New York: Paulist Press, 1997), 571.

3. "Blessed are those who are persecuted for righteousness' sake, for theirs is the kingdom of heaven. Blessed are you when people revile you and persecute you and utter all kinds of evil against you falsely on my account. Rejoice and be glad, for your reward is great in heaven, for in the same way they persecuted the prophets who were before you" (Matt 5:10-11).

4. See Donald Senior, *The Passion of Jesus Christ* (Totowa, NJ: Catholic Book Publishing Co., 1997), 96. The charism of his religious community is the Passion of Our Lord. This little book takes each of the four gospels and gives the perspective of each evangelist. For further study on the passion narrative, refer to his bibliography, which is in three sections: (1) The Historical Setting of the Passion; (2) Archeological Studies; and (3) On the Passion in the New Testament.

5. This is René Girard's term for channeling hostility onto a victim to achieve relative stability and peace. See Leo Lefebure,

Revelation, the Religions, and Violence (Maryknoll, NY: Orbis Books, 2000), 225.

Chapter 3

1. Thirteenth Revelation, chapter 27. This is quoted in the section under "Divine Providence" in *Catechism of the Catholic Church*, 2nd ed. (Vatican City: Libreria Editrice Vaticana, 1992), par. 313.

2. I asked Catherine Hindle, a physician from Wales whose work involves caring for the dying, to read this chapter. She responded: "For me there has always been a clear 'before' of continued living and 'after' of death. Before the person, even if unconscious, is still present but after there remains nothing of the essence—they have clearly gone beyond our ability to experience their personhood any longer. Even in great suffering, the natural end is gentle."

Chapter 4

1. Sandra Schneiders, *Jesus Risen in Our Midst: Essays on the Resurrection of Jesus in the Fourth Gospel* (Collegeville, MN: Liturgical Press, 2013), 146.

2. Julian of Norwich, *Revelations of Divine Love* (New York: Penguin Books, 1966):

> So it was that I learned that love was our Lord's meaning. And I saw for certain, both here and elsewhere, that before ever he made us, God loved us; and that his love has never slackened, nor ever shall. In this love all his works have been done, and in this love he has made everything serve us; and in this love our life is everlasting. Our beginning was when we were made, but the love in which he made us never had beginning. In it we have our beginning.

All this we shall see in God for ever. May Jesus grant this. Amen.
(chap. 86, p. 212)

3. Schneiders, *Jesus Risen in Our Midst*, 96.

4. Raymond E. Brown, *The Gospel According to John*, AB 29 (Garden City, NY: Doubleday, 1966), 133.

5. I am using this term deliberately to point to both the Lord's presence in the Old Testament tabernacle and the covering over, lifting, and consecration in the case of Mary at the annunciation.

6. A guide for me in writing this book has been to avoid apologetics. While there is a place and time for disputes and truth claims, the voice of this book is to simply raise up what can be retrieved from tradition, reclaimed, and reappropriated for our times. The wrath of God, anger of Jesus, and juridical church militant can foster reaction rather than discerned response. I have found in John's gospel to be this explicit revelation of love. I realize there are other traditions at work in our Christian legacy. Given the current "new normal" of violence being the status quo, this message of love is particularly compelling.

7. I underestimated the weight of prevailing theories and legitimation for violence. It seems that we have much work to do to raise up cogent thinking that avoids the pitfalls of just war theory, how passivism evokes violence, and simplistic application of gospel mandates in actual historical situations that require skillful response and common sense. There are two major problems, it seems to me. The first is a literal reading of Scripture that uses only the logical senses. Second, the complexity of violence that has been at work for centuries and the patient and long-suffering ways to deal with the suffering. In 1999, the Monastic Interreligious Dialogue Board sponsored a second Gethsemani Encounter, with the topic being suffering. The conclusion: we

need to heal those who are suffering; if we can't heal, then we should accompany them; if we can't reduce their suffering, then we should work on their behalf and do our best to prevent their suffering. If we cannot heal, prevent, or accompany, then we should teach how to transmute suffering through inner practice (like the Little Way of St. Therese of Lisieux).

Chapter 5

1. Jesus entered into actual time. The reversal of violence belongs to the realm of revelation that is not yet available to ordinary senses. That we know this is so is enough for the realm of faith.

2. Works on the nature of violence and religion include René Girard, *The Girard Reader*, ed. James G. Williams (New York: Crossroad, 1996) and René Girard, *Violence and the Sacred* (Baltimore: Johns Hopkins University Press, 1972). The book I found most helpful of the nine books written by René Girard is *I See Satan Fall Like Lightning*, trans. James G. Williams (Maryknoll, NY: Orbis Books, 2001). For a summary and critique, see Leo D. Lefebure, *Revelation, the Religions, and Violence* (Maryknoll, NY: Orbis Books, 2000), 16–23. Also, Leo D. Lefebure, *True and Holy: Christian Scripture and Other* Religions (Maryknoll, NY: Orbis Books, 2014). It was a difficult choice to limit this book on renouncing violence to the practice of renouncing rather than be a teaching on the contemporary and insightful theories of violence. If the reader of this book is so inclined, the writings of Professor Leo Lefebure and the late Professor René Girard are highly recommended. Another road not taken in the scope of this book was to bring forward the legacy of Thomas Merton and his compelling contemplative voice about nonviolence. For fur-

ther study, I recommend William H. Shannon, *Seeds of Peace* (New York: Crossroads, 1966). Shannon's works cited is comprehensive and includes a lifetime of research.

3. Julian of Norwich's *Revelations of Divine Love* is a treasured text that expresses this spirituality of confidence that all shall be well; see Julian of Norwich, *Showings*, trans. Edmund Colledge and James Walsh (New York: Paulist Press, 1978). For the highest tribute to Julian of Norwich, note the preface written by Benedictine monk Jean Leclercq while he was at Fordham University in 1977.

4. Mary Margaret Funk, *Into the Depths: A Journey of Loss and Vocation* (New York: Lantern Books, 2011), 99.

5. I'm aware that feminist circles would refrain from the use of the word "Lord" because of its patriarchal allusions. Yet, as an English-speaking Benedictine, I have not found another English word that fits my experience of deference, reverence, and interpersonal relationship.

6. For further discussion, see Yves Congar, *I Believe in the Holy Spirit* (New York: Crossroad, 1997).

7. See chapter 6 in my *Lectio Matters: Before the Burning Bush* (Collegeville, MN: Liturgical Press, 2013), 172–94.

8. For further examples of discernment as a practice, see my book, *Discernment Matters* (Collegeville, MN: Liturgical Press, 2013).

Chapter 6

1. The content of the dispute isn't the teaching here, so I'm not divulging the story. Cassian teaches that the content of anger matters not. It is as harmful to have a little thin piece of foil over the eyes as it is blinding to have a thick plank. I include a comprehensive introduction to Cassian's teaching on the affliction of

anger in *Thoughts Matter: Discovering the Spiritual Journey* (Collegeville, MN: Liturgical Press, 2013), 79–103. Each of the five books in the Matters series has a chapter on anger.

Chapter 7

1. We also must accept that this is so. Again, Julian of Norwich says we'll see the "why" later from the other side and see that sin and suffering are beneficial to each of us.

2. When writing *Thoughts* and *Tools* of the Matters series, I was executive director of Monastic Interreligious Dialogue. This gave me the opportunity to teach alongside other Eastern traditions that had a theory of practice of training of the mind. This dialogue was a rigorous immersion into wisdom traditions. In this book, I have brought forward the early contemplative tradition that was the written teachings from the Desert Elders.

3. Refer to the bibliography for the five books in the Matters series, revised and published by Liturgical Press in 2013.

4. Evagrius of Pontus, *Talking Back: A Monastic Handbook for Combating Demons*, trans. David Brackke (Collegeville, MN: Liturgical Press, 2009).

5. The inner journey, the contemplative life, has many traditions lifted up through the ages by writers like Origen, Cassian, Basil, Gregory of Nyssa, John Climacus, Theresa of Avila, John of the Cross, Thérèse of Lisieux to name a few. The journey is toward God. In the seeking, God abides. There is a pattern of ongoing conversion that converges with the destination. Presence precedes.

6. In Cassian, he distinctly says that the cause of violence need not determine the response. When angry, one cannot pray. In the case of dejection that causes depression, it is helpful to determine the source and temper the response according to the cause. For

more on the relationship between anger and prayer, see Gabriel Bunge, *Dragon's Wine and Angel's Bread: The Teaching of Evagrius Ponticus on Anger and Meekness*, trans. Anthony P. Gythiel (Crestwood, NY: St. Vladimir's Seminary Press, 2009).

7. First published as Mary Margaret Funk, "Just What Is the Sabbath?," *Give Us This Day: Daily Prayer for Today's Catholic* 7, no. 7 (July 2017): 301–2.

8. The earliest tradition of Sabbath was rest, as in refraining from work. Notice in Genesis that God rested from work on the seventh day. The observance was to rest. It was later and especially a Christian interpretation that conflated this resting with worship, as in liturgy (literally means "work of the people"). Perhaps it's time to unlink the Sabbath from liturgy, so we can retrieve the original intent, "to rest."

9. *Conversatio morum.* There's not an English translation for this ongoing habitual practice of turning, of conversion, toward God. The term "seeking God" comes close to how it feels from the inside.

10. Pope Francis has dedicated his pontificate to extending mercy. In 2013 he declared the Extraordinary Jubilee of Mercy. See the papal bull *Misericordiae Vultus.* For an interview with Pope Francis on how this Holy Year came about, see Pope Francis, *The Name of God Is Mercy: A Conversation with Andrea Tornielli*, trans. Oonagh Stransky (New York: Random House, 2016).

11. For a full teaching on sustained *lectio*, see my *Lectio Matters: Listening with the Ear of the Heart* (Collegeville, MN: Liturgical Press, 2013).

12. The two books that are most helpful to use for spiritual direction that relieves afflictions are my *Thoughts Matter* (Collegeville, MN: Liturgical Press, 2013) and *Tools Matter* (Collegeville, MN: Liturgical Press, 2013). These two books are two sides of the

same coin. One needs the diagnosis (*Thoughts Matter*) and the antidote (*Tools Matter*).

13. See my *Lectio Matters.*

14. See my *Discernment Matters* (Collegeville, MN: Liturgical Press, 2013).

15. In Heathrow Airport, London, there's a sign on the walking sidewalk saying, "Face the direction you are going."

Chapter 8

1. *The Roman Missal* (Vatican City State, 2008), 1026, and *Book of Blessings* (Collegeville, MN: Liturgical Press, 1989), 519–22.

2. For an in-depth discussion of the nature of evil and our response to it based on René Girard's thought, see James Alison, *Jesus the Forgiving Victim: Listening for the Unheard Voice* (Glenview, IL: Doers Publishing, 2013), loc 432 of 6318, Kindle.

Select Bibliography

The Art of Prayer: An Orthodox Anthology. Compiled by Igumen Chariton of Valamo. Translated by E. Kadloubovsky and E. M. Palmer. Edited by Timothy Ware. London: Faber and Faber, 1966.

Athanasius. *The Life of Anthony and the Letter to Marcellinus.* Translated by Robert C. Gregg. Classics of Western Spirituality. New York: Paulist Press, 1980.

Benedict of Nursia. *RB 1980: The Rule of St. Benedict in Latin and English.* Edited by Timothy Fry. Collegeville, MN: Liturgical Press, 1981.

———. *Benedict's Rule: A Translation and Commentary.* Translated by Terrence Kardong. Collegeville, MN: Liturgical Press, 1996.

———. *The Rule of Benedict: An Invitation to the Christian Life.* Commentary by Georg Holzherr. Translated by Mark Thamert. Collegeville, MN: Liturgical Press, 2016.

Bernard of Clairvaux. *A Lover Teaching the Way of Love: Selected Spiritual Writings.* Edited by M. Basil Pennington. New York: New City Press, 1997.

Bianchi, Enzo. *Praying the Word: An Introduction to* Lectio Divina. Translated by James W. Zona. Cistercian Studies 182. Kalamazoo, MI: Cistercian Publications, 1998.

Billy, Dennis J. *The Way of the Pilgrim: Complete Text and Reader's Guide.* Liguori, MO: Liguori Publications, 2000.

The Book of the Elders: Sayings of the Desert Fathers; The Systematic Collection. Translated by John Wortley. Collegeville, MN: Liturgical Press, 2012.

Bossis, Gabrielle. *He and I.* Translated and condensed by Evelyn M. Brown Sherbrooke. Quebec: Mediaspaul 1969.

Breck, John. *Scripture in Tradition: The Bible and Its Interpretation in the Orthodox Church.* Crestwood, NY: St. Vladimir's Seminary Press, 2001.

Brother Lawrence of the Resurrection. *The Practice of the Presence of God.* Edited by Hal M. Helms. Translated by Robert J. Edmonson. Brewster, MA: Paraclete Press, 1985.

Casey, Michael. *Sacred Reading: The Art of* Lectio Divina. Liguori, MO: Triumph Books, 1995.

————. *Seventy-Four Tools for Good Living: Reflections on the Fourth Chapter of Benedict.* Collegeville, MN: Liturgical Press, 2014.

————. *Toward God: The Ancient Wisdom of Western Prayer.* Rev. ed. Liguori, MO: Triumph Books, 1996.

Cassian, John. *The Conferences.* Translated by Boniface Ramsey. Ancient Christian Writers 57. New York: Newman / Paulist Press, 1997.

————. *The Institutes.* Translated by Boniface Ramsey. Ancient Christian Writers 58. New York: Newman / Paulist Press, 2000.

Clément, Olivier. *The Roots of Christian Mysticism: Text and Commentary.* Translated by Theodore Berkeley and Jeremy Hummerstone. New York: New City Press, 1995.

Climacus, John. *The Ladder of Divine Ascent.* Translated by Colm Luibheid and Norman Russell. Classics of Western Spirituality. New York: Paulist Press, 1982.

The Cloud of Unknowing and the Book of Privy Counseling. Edited by William Johnston. Garden City, NY: Image Books, 1973.

Cummings, Charles. *Monastic Practices.* Cistercian Studies 75. Kalamazoo, MI: Cistercian Publications, 1986; rev. ed., Monastic Wisdom 47, 2015.

de Lubac, Henri. *Medieval Exegesis: The Four Senses of Scripture.* Vols. 1 and 2. Grand Rapids, MI: William B. Eerdmans Publishing, 1998.

The Desert Fathers: Translations from the Latin Verbum Senorium. Translated by Helen Waddell. Ann Arbor: University of Michigan Press, 1957.

Evagrius Ponticus. *Ad Monachos.* Translation and commentary by Jeremy Driscoll. Ancient Christian Writers 59. New York: Newman Press, 2003.

———. *The Mind's Long Journey to the Holy Trinity: The* Ad Monachos *of Evagrius Ponticus.* Translated by Jeremy Driscoll. Collegeville, MN: Liturgical Press, 1994.

———. *The* Praktikos *and Chapters on Prayer.* Translated by John Eudes Bamberger. Cistercian Studies 4. Kalamazoo, MI: Cistercian Publications, 1972.

———. *Talking Back:* Antirrhetikos; *A Monastic Handbook for Combating Demons.* Translated by David Brakke. Collegeville, MN: Liturgical Press, 2009.

Funk, Mary Margaret. *Discernment Matters: Listening with the Ear of the Heart.* Collegeville MN: Liturgical Press, 2013.

———. *Humility Matters: Toward Purity of Heart.* Collegeville, MN: Liturgical Press, 2013.

―――. *Lectio Matters: Before the Burning Bush*. Collegeville, MN: Liturgical Press, 2013.

―――. *Thoughts Matter: Discovering the Spiritual Journey*. Collegeville, MN: Liturgical Press, 2013.

―――. *Tools Matter: Beginning the Spiritual Journey*. Collegeville, MN: Liturgical Press, 2013.

Gillette, Gertrude. *The Four Faces of Anger: Seneca, Evagrius, Cassian, and Augustine*. Lanham, MD: University Press of America, 2010.

Gregory of Nyssa. *The Life of Moses*. Translated by Abraham J. Malherbe and Everett Ferguson. Classics of Western Spirituality. New York: Paulist Press, 1978.

Guigo II. *Ladder of Monks and Twelve Meditations*. Translated by Edmund Colledge and James Walsh. Cistercian Studies 48. Kalamazoo, MI: Cistercian Publications, 1981.

Harmless, William. *Desert Christians: An Introduction to the Literature of Early Monasticism*. New York: Oxford University Press, 2004.

Hausherr, Irenee. *The Name of Jesus*. Translated by Charles Cummings. Cistercian Studies 44. Kalamazoo, MI: Cistercian Publications, 1978.

―――. *Penthos: The Doctrine of Compunction in the Christian East*. Translated by Anselm Hufstader. Cistercian Studies 53. Kalamazoo, MI: Cistercian Publications, 1982.

―――. *Spiritual Direction in the Early Christian East*. Translated by Anthonly P. Gythiel. Cistercian Studies 116. Kalamazoo, MI: Cistercian Publications, 1990.

Julian of Norwich. *Julian of Norwich: Showings*. Translated and edited by Edmund Colledge and James Walsh. New York: Paulist Press, 1978.

Leclercq, Jean. *The Love of Learning and the Desire for God: A Study of Monastic Culture.* Translated by Catherine Misrahi. New York: Fordham University Press, 1961.

The Life of Saint Pachomius and His Disciples. Translated by Armand Veilleux. Vol. 1 of Pachomian Koinonia. Cistercian Studies 45. Kalamazoo, MI: Cistercian Publications, 1980.

Lives of the Desert Fathers: The Historia Monachorum in Aegypto. Translated by Norman Russell. Cistercian Studies 34. Kalamazoo, MI: Cistercian Publications, 1981.

McGinn, Bernard. *The Presence of God: A History of Western Christian Mystery.* Vol. 1: *The Foundations of Mysticism: Origins to the Fifth Century.* New York: Crossroads, 1991.

Merton, Thomas. *The Climate of Monastic Prayer.* Cistercian Studies 1. Kalamazoo, MI: Cistercian Publications, 1973; new ed., Collegeville, MN: Liturgical Press, 2018.

Palladius. *The Lausiac History.* Translated by Robert T. Meyer. Ancient Christian Writers 4. New York: Paulist Press, 1965.

Pelikan, Jaroslav. *Whose Bible Is It? A Short History of the Scriptures.* New York: Penguin Books, 2005.

Philokalia: The Complete Text. Vols. 1–4. Compiled by St. Nikodimos of the Holy Mountain and St. Makarios of Corinth. Translated and edited by G. E. H. Palmer, Philip Sherrad, and Kallistos Ware. London: Faber and Faber, 1979–1995.

Robertson, Duncan. *Lectio Divina: The Medieval Experience of Reading.* Collegeville, MN: Liturgical Press, 2011.

Rolf, Veronica Mary. *Julian's Gospel: Illuminating the Life and Revelations of Julian of Norwich.* Maryknoll, NY: Orbis Books, 2013.

The Sayings of the Desert Fathers: The Alphabetical Collection. Translated by Benedicta Ward. Cistercian Studies 59. Kalamazoo, MI: Cistercian Publications, 1975.

Schneiders, Sandra. *Jesus Risen in Our Midst: Essays on the Resurrection of Jesus in the Fourth Gospel.* Collegeville, MN: Liturgical Press, 2013.

———. *The Revelatory Text.* San Francisco: Harper, 1991.

———. "Scripture and Spirituality." In *Christian Spirituality: Origins to the Twelfth Century*, edited by Bernard McGinn, J. Meyendorff, and Jean Leclercq. New York: Fortress Press, 1985.

———. *Written That You May Believe: Encountering Jesus in the Fourth Gospel.* 2nd ed. New York: Crossroads, 2003.

Spidlik, Thomas. *The Spirituality of the Christian East: A Systematic Handbook.* 2 vols. Translated by Anthony P. Gythiel. Cistercian Studies 79. Kalamazoo, MI: Cistercian Publications, 1986.

Stewart, Columba. *Cassian the Monk.* New York: Oxford University Press, 1998.

Studzinski, Raymond. *Reading to Live: The Evolving Practice of Lectio Divina.* Cistercian Studies 231. Collegeville, MN: Cistercian Publications, 2009.

Teresa of Avila. *The Way of Perfection: A Study Edition.* Edited by Kieran Kavanaugh. Translated by Kieran Kavanaugh and Otilio Rodriguez. Washington, DC: ICS Publications, 2000.

Thérèse of Lisieux. *Story of a Soul: The Autobiography of St. Thérèse of Lisieux.* Translated by John Clark. 3rd ed. Washington, DC: ICS Publications, 1996.

Turner, Denys. *Julian of Norwich, Theologian.* New Haven, CT: Yale University Press, 2011.

Ward, Benedicta. *Harlots of the Desert: A Study of Repentance in Early Monastic Sources.* Collegeville, MN: Cistercian Publications, 1987.

The Wisdom of the Desert. Compiled by Thomas Merton. New York: New Directions, 1960.